# The Craft of Printing
## and the
## Publication of Shakespeare's Works

FRONTISPIECE
The English common press. This press, now in the Smithsonian Institution, Washington, D.C., was used in a London print shop throughout the eighteenth century; in all significant respects, it is identical to the kind of press perfected by Gutenberg and used by Caxton and the printers of Shakespeare's works. According to a pleasant tradition, Benjamin Franklin is said to have learned the trade of printer on this press in London in 1726. (Photograph reproduced through the kind permission of the Smithsonian Institution.)

*To* Fredson Bowers

# Contents

# Illustrations

# Acknowledgments

I should like to express my particular thanks for their assistance to Miss Elizabeth Harris at the Smithsonian Institution, to the Reverend Doctor John L. Sharpe, III, at the Duke University Library, to Sra. Martha M. de Narváez at the Hispanic Society of America, to Miss Katharine F. Pantzer of the Short-Title Catalogue at the Houghton Library, and to these friends at the Folger Shakespeare Library: Megan Lloyd, who persuaded me to begin this project, Giles Dawson who assisted me on it, and John Andrews who encouraged me to finish it.

General thanks also to the staffs of the reference collections and the photographic divisions at the British Library, the Smithsonian Institution, the Hispanic Society of America, the Folger Shakespeare Library, the Henry E. Huntington Library, the New York Public Library, and the libraries at Duke, Williams, and Yale for courtesies over the years as well as during the preparation of this pamphlet.

Special thanks finally to Fredson Bowers who confirmed my interests in the craft of printing and in the publication of Shakespeare's works.

# The Craft of Printing
## and the
## Publication of Shakespeare's
## Works

# [ 1 ]

# The Invention of Printing

The engraved title page for a volume describing "New Discoveries" *(Nova Reperta),* published in Antwerp about A.D. 1600, depicts as its central "discovery" a printing press (plate 2). On either side of this press are representations of the New World and of a compass ("lapis polaris"). These three discoveries seemed to the artist, Jan van der Straet, three of the most significant accomplishments of Renaissance invention; they symbolized the conquests of time and of space. For just as the discovery of the New World, the newfound land, was a conquest of space, so surely was the discovery of printing a conquest of time. As Renaissance mind and spirit extended themselves into the new hemisphere, so did they extend themselves into the future.

The first printers recognized immediately that they were conquerors of time, and they saw themselves as conferring immortality on the works of others even as they accepted the limitations of their own mortality. The earliest known pictorial representation of a printing press is that in *La grant dans macabre* (The great dance of death) published in Lyons in 1499 (see plate 3). It shows three skeletal figures of Death, clutching a compositor, a pressman, and a bookseller in the midst of their work. A French illustration of a press in *La Fauconnerie de messire Arthelouche,* published in Poitiers in 1567 has two mottoes: *vitam mortuo reddo* ("I restore life from death") and *Je ravie le mort* ("I despoil death"). A comparable scene appears in a later English representation of a press, in *The Booke of Christian Prayers* published in London in 1578. A motto appears on this illustration:

We Printers wrote with wisedome's pen:
She lives for aye, we die as men.

Plate 2
Title page, *Nova Reperta* (Antwerp, ca. 1600). The engraving by Joannus Stradanus (Jan van der Straet) shows the printing press with stacks of paper and ink balls, and with printed sheets hanging up to dry. (Courtesy of the Folger Shakespeare Library.)

The description of the printing press in the *Nova Reperta* (plate 4) carries the motto: "Potest ut una vox capi aure plurima: Linunt ita una scripta mille paginas" (As a single voice can capture many through the ear, so a single writing spreads over a thousand copies). Before the invention of writing, the ideas of humankind were transmitted orally from person to person—from Homer to his hearers, from Socrates and Jesus to their disciples—but it was always evident that human memories were fragile channels through which to transmit the words of those departed, and hearers and disciples have written down such words before they forgot them, knowing well that a short note was better than a long memory. Nevertheless, a single such record was itself subject to decay, destruction, or loss. Though writing centuries later and in recent times, Thomas Jefferson has described this problem and this battle against time:

In the course of my researches into the laws of Virginia, I observed that many of them were already lost, and many more on the point of being lost, as existing only in single copies in the hands of careful . . . individuals, on whose deaths they would probably be used for waste paper. I set myself therefore to work to collect all which were then existing. . . . But [when once I have collected them] what means will be the most effectual for preserving these remains from future loss . . . from the worm, from the natural decay of the paper, from the accident of fire . . .? Our experience has proved to us that a single copy, or a few deposited in manuscript in the public offices cannot be relied on for any great length of time.

[Laws and records will be saved] not by vaults and locks which fence them from the public eye and use . . . , but by such a

Plate 3

Woodcut from *La grant dans macabre* (Lyons: Mathias Huss, 1499). Figures of Death clutching compositor at his cases, pressman at the press, bookseller in his shop, and an apprentice, defending himself with an ink ball. (Reproduced through the kind permission of the British Library.)

IMPRESSIO LIBRORVM.
*Potest vt vna vox capi aure plurima :        Linunt ita vna scripta mille paginas .*

Plate 4

Impressio Librorum (The printing of books), *Nova Reperta* (Antwerp, ca. 1600). The print shop—three compositors, one proofreader (with spectacles), a porter bringing in a stack of paper, one pressman inking the type and another taking the impression, an apprentice stacking sheets of printed paper, and the master printer. In the distant background center, the city clock. (Courtesy of the Folger Shakespeare Library.)

  multiplication of copies, as shall place them beyond the reach of accident.*

Jefferson understood that effective preservation lay not in protection but in proliferation, not in keeping from the public but in distributing to the public—spreading a single writing over a thousand copies. The method of distributing to the public—of publication—was in his day the printing press, which made possible, as Jefferson specified in another passage, "a multiplication of printed copies."

---

*Thomas Jefferson to George Wythe, 16 January 1796; to Ebenezer Hazard, 18 February 1791, quoted in Julian P. Boyd, "'These Precious Monuments of our History,'" *American Archivist* 22 (April 1959): 175–76.

Before the invention of the machines that could transform a single manuscript into thousands of printed copies, the only way to make books public was to write them individually by hand, one copy at a time. This labor was performed by scribes, who copied out a text letter by letter.* As an individual scribe might copy a manuscript before his eyes and so transmit one copy to the future, in large "publishing houses" many scribes might simultaneously copy a manuscript that was read aloud, the single voice of the reader filling the ears of the many scribes. This sort of publication—at best slow, costly, and tedious—is possible only in a society in which human labor is cheap. Historically, the societies producing multiple copies of manuscripts were those of classical Greece and Rome, of ancient Egypt, and of the medieval Christian church.

The transmission of texts by manuscript was not only slow, costly, and tedious; it was also selective and subject to human error. It was selective in so far as only the best texts (or those considered the best) were thought worthy of the attention and diligence necessary to write them down, and to write them down time and time again as individual copies wore out or perished by fire or sword. (The youthful student of the literature of ancient Greece no doubt deplores the large number of texts that he must master; he may console himself with the thought that only 2 percent of that literature has survived.) It was subject to human error; every copy of every manuscript—those produced singly and those produced in quantity—passed through the memory and hands of a fallible mortal.

The energy of the fifteenth century required that ever-increasing amounts of information and experience be made available in accurate form to an ever-increasing number of literate people throughout civilized Europe, and the inventiveness of humanity responded to that challenge by discovering how to print with movable types. The ease with which a book could be printed and disseminated put an end to the selectivity of the old system; and though readers of the fifteenth century complained—as do readers of today—that much being printed in books was neither needful nor fit to print, having too much from which to select is surely preferable to having too little.

Similarly, though error is a part of the human condition, multiple copies of a published print, unlike multiple copies of a published manuscript, were very nearly identical, and future editions remaining uniform in text could be successively corrected and freed from

---

*It is still performed with a holy and exacting zeal in the preparation of the sacred scrolls of the Torah.

mechanical or careless error. "Textual drift" was arrested, and modern editing was born.

In the first half of the fifteenth century, "inventors" at Avignon, Bruges, Bologna, Haarlem, and Strasbourg were directing their minds toward various techniques of producing "artificial script"— that is, writing made by the means of art (or skill). One technique that these early inventors attempted was printing by blocks, or "xylography." This process developed from the custom of printing illustrations that had been carved on blocks of wood. Now, if it was possible to print illustrations carved on blocks of wood, it would be equally possible to print words carved on blocks of wood. Accordingly, xylographers with some success carved pages of text on wood blocks, printed the pages, and bound up the printed pages as books. Of one xylographer, Laurens Janszoon Coster of Haarlem, is told the pleasant legend that in the 1440s, he carved not pages of solid text but individual letters on individual blocks of wood—movable wooden types, so to speak—and with them printed books to help his grandchildren learn to read.

Though xylography was a useful technique (and still is for special printing purposes), it was limited by the characteristics of its materials; and, though it could supply the educational needs of a small domestic circle, it could not be perfected to supply the educational needs of Renaissance Europe. The technique that could fulfill those needs was the technique of printing with movable metal types.

There is now general agreement that the invention of printing in Western Civilization should be attributed to Johann Gensfleisch zum Gutenberg, a patrician of Mainz (1394–1468), and to him alone. But, as one historian has observed, though it is easy to say that Gutenberg invented printing, it is not so easy to define what that invention actually was; for the invention of printing depended not on the contrivance of a single mechanical device but on the development of several devices, techniques, and elements and on the synthesis of them all.

The problems that Gutenberg had to solve before inventing the art of printing with movable types were many and various. Their solution required a command of what we should now call mechanical engineering, physics, graphics, gemcutting, metallurgy, and chemistry. In each of these separate fields Gutenberg, working with familiar tools and techniques, achieved a brilliant adaptation that served his particular purposes. His greatest achievement, however, lay not in these various inventions but in the inspiration through which he fused them all into the service of a new technology. Gutenberg did not invent the idea of printing from movable types; what he invented was the process by which printing from movable types was practicable.

Gutenberg began the preliminary work for the invention of printing in the late 1430s or the early 1440s in Strasbourg, where he had gone after the tradesmen and citizens, in 1428, had succeeded in depriving the patricians of their special privileges in Mainz. He worked in secret, as various documents of this part of his career testify, and, after returning to Mainz in the late 1440s, continued the development of his technology. In 1450 the patrician Gutenberg borrowed 800 guilders from the citizen Johannes Fust. Two years later he borrowed another 800 guilders, on the condition that Fust be admitted to the secret. We must suppose that in this period Gutenberg perfected his invention in its many parts; he certainly was operating what we should now call a print shop with a considerable investment in equipment and several employees. One of these, his foreman, Peter Schöffer, seems to have been a better printer and typographer even than Gutenberg was.

From Gutenberg's print shop, several samples of printing survive that can be dated to the first half of the decade of the 1450s: a scrap of a *Sibyllenbuch* (a long poem on the Last Judgment), pieces of schoolbooks, calendars, and forms for Papal Indulgences. The earliest piece of printing with a positive date is an Indulgence of 1454. But these were trifles in comparison to the great work that Gutenberg, Fust, and Schöffer were preparing—the unprecedented undertaking of the printing of the Bible. This heretofore inconceivable project involved four to six presses, many workmen, large amounts of paper and vellum, and substantial capital. In November 1455, however, as the work was nearing completion, history repeated itself: Fust, the citizen, foreclosed on Gutenberg, the patrician, depriving him of his rights in the product of his own inventiveness and ousting him from the firm. The great Bible, now generally called the "Gutenberg Bible," was published by the firm of Fust and Schöffer in 1455 or early 1456 (plate 5).

Gutenberg, Fust, Schöffer—inventor, financier, artist—might have formed an ideal working trio, but we do not live in an ideal world. Fust and Schöffer continued to operate the printing house; Gutenberg left the city.

In 1457 Fust and Schöffer published, in Mainz, a *Psalterium,* a magnificent work with initials printed in blue and red ink (not hand illuminated) and with music for chanting the psalms—a masterpiece of printing. Their firm published steadily for many years, maintaining high standards. Gutenberg printed a second Bible, perhaps in Bamberg in 1458–59; and in 1460, in a second printery in Mainz, he

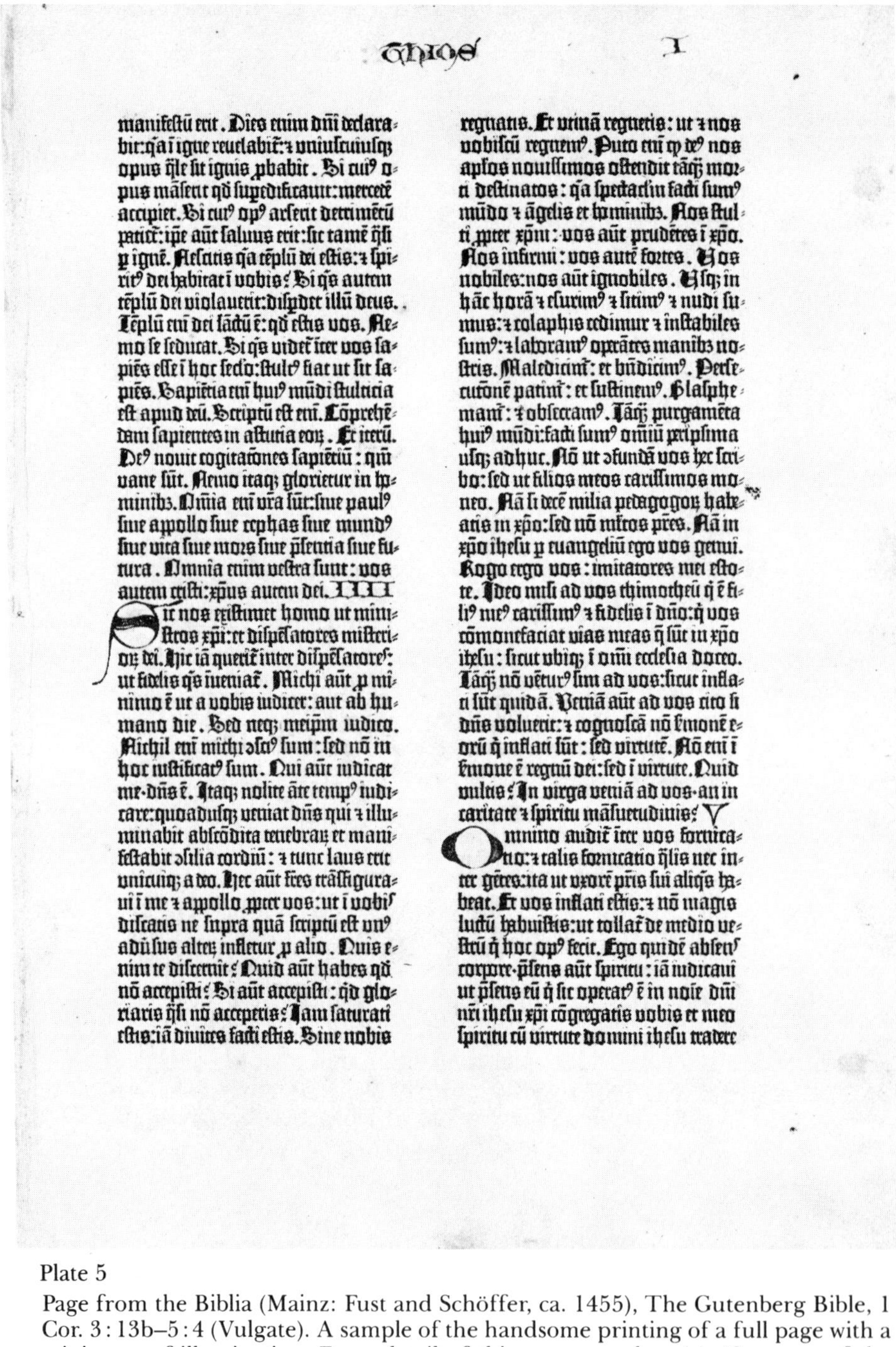

Plate 5

Page from the Biblia (Mainz: Fust and Schöffer, ca. 1455), The Gutenberg Bible, 1 Cor. 3 : 13b–5 : 4 (Vulgate). A sample of the handsome printing of a full page with a minimum of illumination. For a detail of this page see plate 14. (Courtesy of the Folger Shakespeare Library.)

presumably published an encyclopedia by Johannes Balbus, *Catholicon,* the colophon to which, translated, reads:

> With the help of the Most High, at whose will the tongues of infants become eloquent and who often reveals to the lowly what he hides from the wise, this noble book, *Catholicon,* has been printed and accomplished without the help of reed, stylus, or pen but by the wondrous agreement, proportion, and harmony of punches and types, in the year of the Lord's incarnation 1460 in the noble city of Mainz.

After this publication—if indeed it is his—Gutenberg disappears from the history of printing. But in a professional career of a scant twenty years, he had accomplished his miracle. He had made it possible for both sacred and secular texts to be disseminated everywhere; he had discovered the mass market; he had invented the "job-printing" business; and he had, to his sorrow, demonstrated the need for capital in publishing ventures. By the spread of a single manuscript over thousands of copies, he had nearly precluded the possibility that recorded ideas could be totally destroyed, and he had thereby assured their survival through time.

> He taught the lever with unceasing play
> To stop the waste of time's destructive sway.

The drama of the achievement at Mainz in the 1450s was electric, and those who had caught the vision of Gutenberg, had learned the skill of his fingers, and had mastered the craft in his shop or in that of Fust and Schöffer went out as missionaries of the printed word to seek their fortunes in the world. Presses were established in Cologne in 1464, in Basel in 1466, in Rome in 1467, in Venice in 1469, in Paris, Utrecht, Milan, Florence, Lyons, Valencia, Budapest, Cracow, Bruges, Westminster, Rostock, Geneva, Pilsen, and London, all before 1480; in Leipzig in 1481, in Odense in 1482, in Stockholm in 1483. The first fifty years of printing—from 1450 to 1500—are termed the *incunabula* period, from the Latin word meaning "in the cradle." But the infant trade was Herculean in its strength; the presses of Western Europe in that period produced over eight million volumes, about one-third of them illustrated—a flood of books such as had never been known in the history of the world.

These volumes hardly differed in their subject matter from those first published by Gutenberg: sacred writ and secular learning. To such topics must be added, of course, the odd-jobs of the printing house, one of the most sustained of which was the printing of Indul-

Plate 6
Title page, Martin Luther, *Resolutiones* (Wittenberg: J. Rhau-Grunenberg, 1518).
Woodcut border by Lucas Cranach, the elder. (Courtesy of the Folger Shakespeare
Library.)

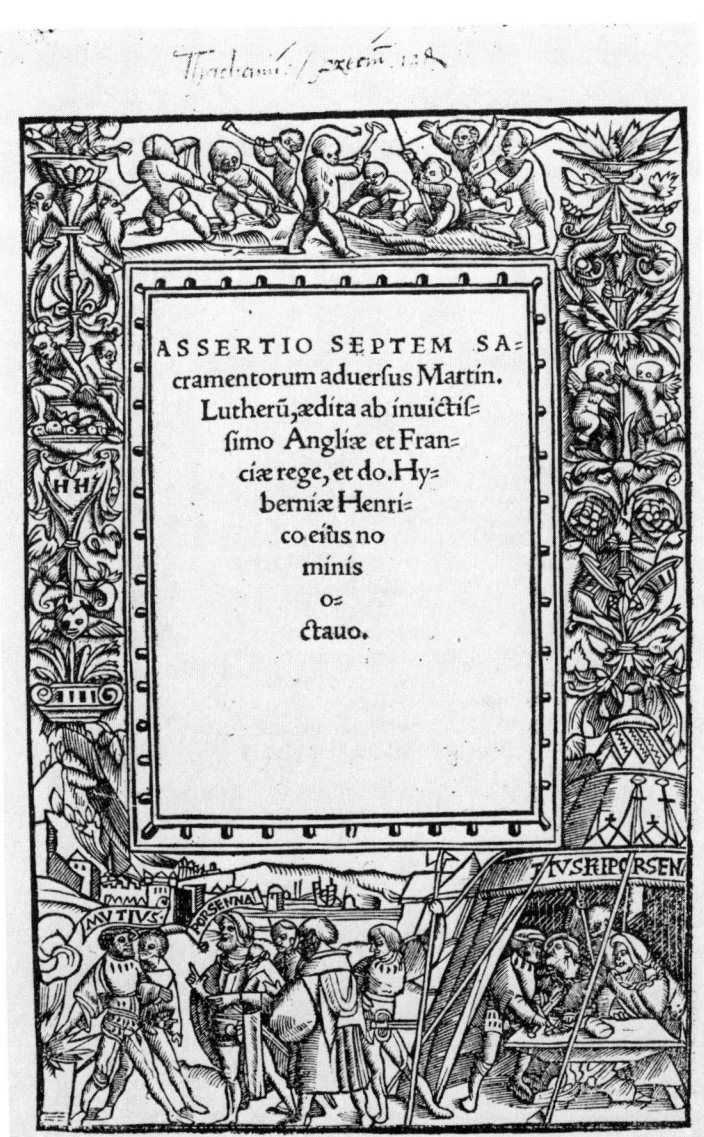

Plate 7

Title page, Henry VIII, *Assertio septem sacramentorum* (London: Richard Pynson, 1521). Title page border by Hans Holbein (signed with initials in the left panel). (Courtesy of the Folger Shakespeare Library.)

Plate 8

Title page, *Dotrina breue muy prouechosa delas cosas que pertenecen a la fe catholica* (Mexico: Juan Cromberger, 1544). First book known to have been printed in America. The text of the title has been inserted in the center of the shield usually reserved for the bishop's coat of arms. The date of the title is "M.dxliij." (1543), the year this first page of the volume was printed or, perhaps more likely, the year the whole volume was supposed to have been printed. (Reproduced from the copy in the Library of the Hispanic Society of America, New York, with the kind permission of the Society.)

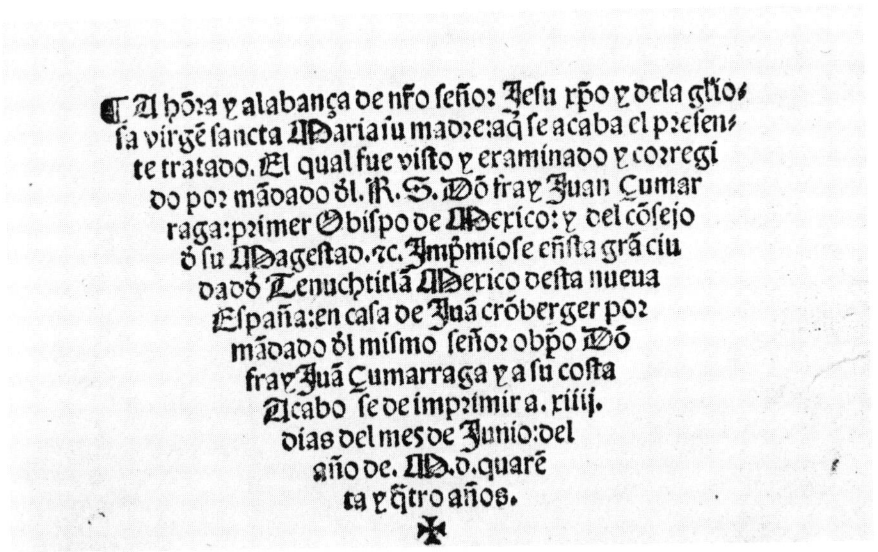

¶ Ahõra y alabança de nõo feñoz Iefu rpo y dela gllos
fa virgé fancta Mariafu madzeaq̃ fe acaba el pzefen
te tratado. El qual fue vifto y eraminado y cozregi
do poz mãdado õl. R. S. Dõ fray Iuan Cumar
raga: pzimer Obifpo de Merico: y del cõfejo
õ fu Mageftad. zc. Impmiofe enfifta grã ciu
dadõ Tenuchtitlã Merico defta nueua
Efpaña: en cafa de Iuã cróberger poz
mãdado õl mifmo feñoz obpo Dõ
fray Iuã Cumarraga y a fu cofta
Acabo fe de impzimir a. riiij.
dias del mes de Iunio: del
año de. M.d.quarẽ
ta y q̃tro años.
✠

Plate 9

Colophon, *Dotrina breue* (Mexico: Juan Cromberger, 1544). The last ten lines may be translated: "Printed in the great city Tenuchtitla*n* Mexico of New Spain: in the house of Jua*n* Cro*m*berger by command of the same Lord Bishop Do*n* Fray Jua*n* Zumarraga and at his cost. Printing was finished on the 14th day of the month of June, in the year of 1544. + ." (Reproduced from the copy in the Library of the Hispanic Society of America, New York, with the kind permission of the Society.)

gences. Just as the earliest dated work from Gutenberg's press was an Indulgence, so the earliest dated work from a press in England was an Indulgence (1476). In 1498, 18,000 Indulgences streamed from a press in Barcelona. Surely it is no accident that Martin Luther is best known for his stand against the sale of Indulgences. His *Ninety-five Theses,* addressing the irregularities in the use of Indulgences, were posted on the door of the Castle Church in Wittenberg in 1517, probably in printed form. Luther turned to printing to communicate his ideas; his *Resolutiones,* supporting the *Theses,* were printed in at least two editions within the next few months (plate 6), and Luther's other writings kept the presses of Wittenberg busy supplying the demand for his work throughout Europe. As one modern scholar has said: "The Reformation flew through Europe on the wings of print." How speedily and how far printed ideas flew throughout Europe we may gather from the record of a scholarly collector who on August 9, 1516, wrote from Bologna to a bookseller in Leipzig—a distance of 500 miles over the Alps and across a

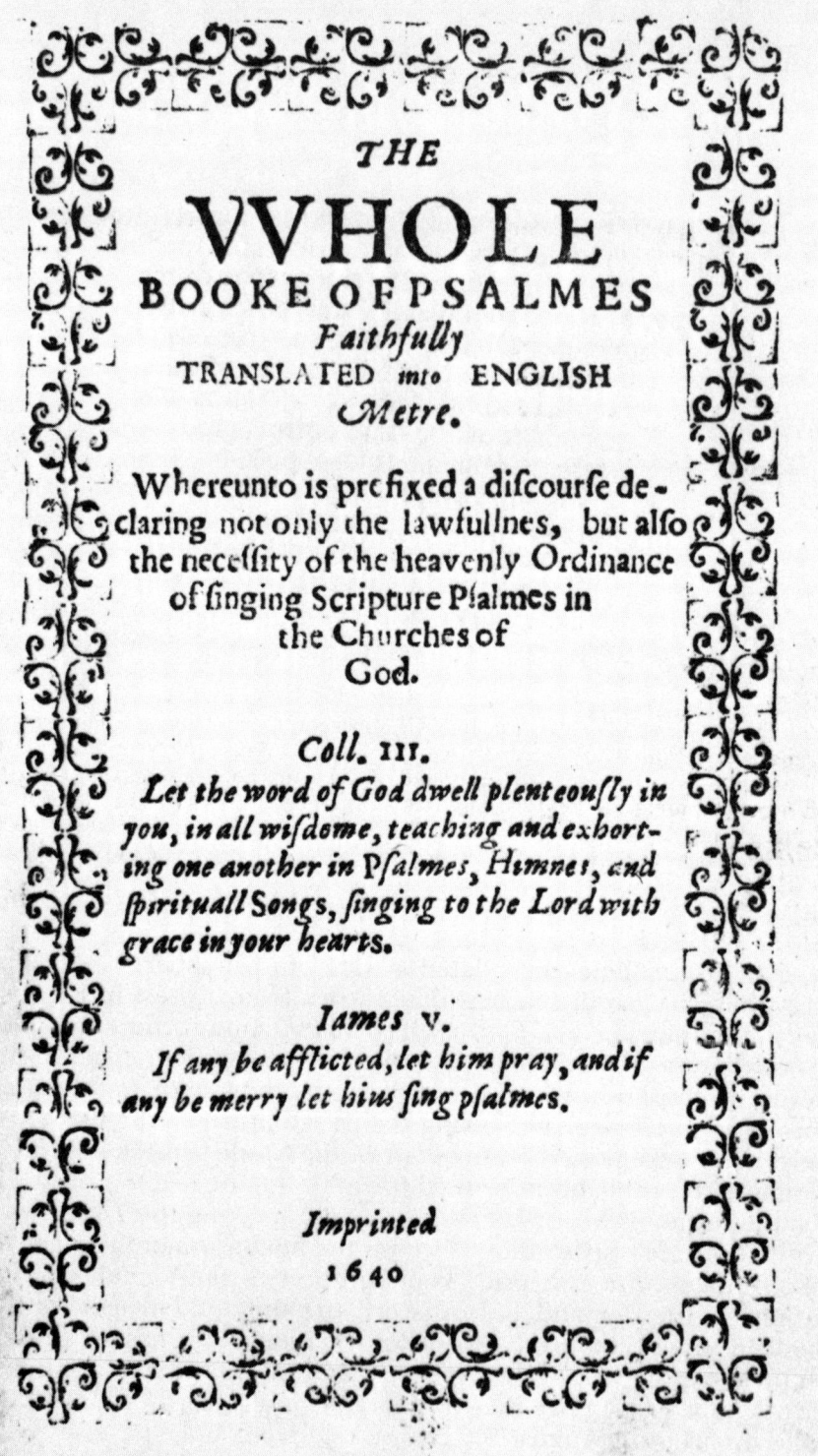

national boundary—to order a book; he received the book on August 22, less than two weeks later. Luther's ideas flew across the English Channel to Henry VIII of England, who replied to them in a Letter to the Pope, published in London in 1521 (plate 7) and reprinted in Augsburg and Rome in succeeding years. The Letter earned for Henry and his descendant kings of England the title "Defensor Fidei" in perpetuity.

Presses moved almost as rapidly as ideas. The first German printers were succeeded by their apprentices of every nation throughout civilized Europe—and beyond; one of these, Juan Cromberger, a Spaniard of German extraction, carried the first press into the New World and erected a printing house in Mexico City, where in 1543–44 he printed the first known American book, *Dotrina breue muy prouechosa delas cosas que pertenecen a la fe catholica* (see plates 8 and 9). A century later, the first press in British America was sent out from Cambridge in England to Cambridge in New England and there set up under the protection of Harvard College; its first known book was the "Bay Psalm Book," printed in 1640 (plate 10).

# [ 2 ]

# The Craft of Printing

## *Printing from Movable Types*

The invention of printing, as has already been suggested, was multiform and various; Gutenberg's great achievement lay in adapting and coordinating traditional techniques to a new and particular process. The most conspicuous element in that coordination was the refinement of the press itself, but more significant in terms of "invention" were the fabrication of the mold to cast the type and the perfection of the formulas for the alloy to make the type metal and the ink to print the type. Though the following sections will treat these and other elements as separate units, they are all interdependent, and, presumably, their development proceeded hand in hand. The great mystery lay in their assimilation into a single function.

### The Press

Gutenberg had before him the problem of developing a mechanism by means of which ink, placed on metal shaped to represent letters, could be transferred from that shaped metal to paper so as to reproduce the design from the metal on the paper. The principle to invoke in effecting such a transfer was pressure. Machines capable of exerting pressure from an upper plate to a lower plate by means of a screw were readily available to Gutenburg. Examples were everywhere at hand: in the home, the linen press; in the fields, the wine press and the olive press; in the trades, the chemist's, the papermaker's, and the bookbinder's presses. All of these devices provided pressure from the upper to the lower plate with a single continuing thrust of long duration through a long transit; what

Gutenberg needed was pressure with many repeated thrusts of brief duration through a short transit. What was new in Gutenberg's design for his press for printing was the ability to provide these many short movements in a day's work instead of one long one: to press a continuing succession of papers, instead of one bag of olives. To accomplish this change, Gutenberg reduced the length of the long screw (characteristic of earlier screw presses and obvious in illustrations of screw presses prior to the printing press) and altered the pitch of its thread.* He thereby reduced the vertical distance to be covered in its descent by the upper plate, or *platen,* of the press and increased the speed of its movement. Furthermore, as the transit of the downward thrust was to be short, the bar to turn the screw could move back and forth in a short arc; it could thus be permanently fixed in the screw and readily operated by a single sturdy pressman. This control of the vertical movement of the platen solved one half of the problem of taking an impression. The second half of the problem—how to bring paper and type together smoothly under the platen—Gutenberg no doubt solved at first simply by placing a sheet of paper on the inked type and sliding type and paper under the platen, lowering the platen, and then pulling them out to replace the printed sheet with a fresh one. An early development facilitated this movement by putting the tray of type on tracks and controlling it by a crank and pulleys. The first English illustration of a printing press appears in the *Ordinary for all Faithfull Christians,* published by Anthony Scoloker in London in 1548 (plate 11). It represents the moment at which the impression is being taken, and it shows clearly the short screw and, in the pressman's left hand, the crank to move the type in and out.

In order to hold the paper steadily in the correct position during the movement of the platen, Gutenberg or his successors contrived the unwieldy but effective device of a frame of two leaves, hinged together, the *frisket* and the *tympan,* both covered with parchment; the parchment in the upper leaf (the frisket) had openings that matched exactly the blocks of type to be printed. These "windows" allowed the inked type to meet the paper but protected the edges of the paper from ink stains and so made possible clean margins for each page on the sheet. When a sheet of paper was to be printed, it was laid on the lower leaf of the frame (the tympan) and fixed on two pins centered on the sides of the tympan; the frisket was then

---

*For example, the thread of the screw is incorrectly drawn in the *Nova Reperta* (plate 4), as if the artist was not aware of the technical distinction; the thread is correctly drawn in the *Grant dans* (plate 3) and in the *Ordinary* (plate 11).

Plate 11
Woodcut from *The ordenarye for all faythfull Chrystians*. . . . Translated out of Doutche into Inglysh by Anthony Scoloker (London or Ipswich: Anthony Scoloker, 1548). Miss Katharine F. Pantzer notes that the cut is printed from the same woodblock used in the Dutch original, printed in Ghent in 1545. (Reproduced with the kind permission of the Chapin Library, Williams College.)

lowered over the paper of the tympan and the whole contraption was folded again over the face of the inked type. Type, frisket, paper, and tympan were then rolled under the platen, and the platen was moved downward by the operation of the pressbar to make the impression. (Because the early platen was small and hence incapable of covering an entire sheet with an even pressure, it was necessary to lower it twice, rolling the type in halfway for the first impression, all the way for the second.) The illustration from Stephen Bateman's *Doom Warning all Men to the Judgment* (London, 1581) shows a side view of the press, and, rising from the right-hand edge of the tray of type, are the tympan and frisket (plate 12; see also plate 13).

Plate 12
Woodcut from Stephen Bateman, *Doom warning all men to the Iudgement* (London: R. Newbery, 1581). (Courtesy of the Folger Shakespeare Library.)

Typographus. Der Buchdrucker.

A Rte mea reliquas illuſtro Typographus artes,
  Imprimo dum varios ære micante libros.
Quæ prius aucta ſitu, quæ puluere plena iacebant,
  Vidimus obſcura nocte ſepulta premi.

Hæc veterum renouo neglecta volumina Patrum
  Atq, ſcolis curo publica facta legi.
Artem prima nouam reperiſſe Moguntia fertur,
  Vrbs grauis, & multis ingenioſa modis.
Qua nihil vtilius videt, aut precioſius orbis,
  Vix melius quicquam ſecla futura dabunt.
                    C 3                Char-

Plate 13
Woodcut, "Printer," from *Panoplia* (Frankfurt: Hartman Schopperum, 1568). (Courtesy of the Folger Shakespeare Library.)

## The Types

When Gutenberg undertook to represent individual letters on individual pieces of metal so that they could be arranged to spell words and then rearranged to spell other words—and the insight to do that is perhaps another of his inventions—he needed to master the skills and arts practiced by various craftsmen. These were, in order of their place in the whole process of making type: the designer, to draw the shape of the letter; the goldsmith (or jeweler or engraver), to cut the letter on a metal punch; the metalworker, to construct a mold in which the pieces of type could be cast; and the metallurgical chemist, to prepare an alloy of the right proportion for use in casting the type. The synthesis of these various skills made possible the production of movable types.

*Designing the Letter.* The designers of the first letters to be used in typography *(typefaces)* had no interest in innovation. They sought to reproduce as best they could in a printed book with their "inferior" mechanical devices the pages of a manuscript book—to produce, as it were, more manuscriptlike books than the best scriptoria could produce. In consequence they aimed no higher and at nothing else than to copy the best forms of letters that literate people could recognize and to which they were accustomed,* and they achieved in their printing a neatness, accuracy, and regularity far beyond those of the normal scribe's ability. The first printed books must have seemed to their purchasers easily the equivalent of the finest scribal work. In the manuscript tradition to which the designers turned, they found different kinds of handwriting, or different styles of lettering, practiced by the professional scribes in satisfying the needs of their various employers (just as in choosing a typewriter today we

---

*In seeking to produce by print a page that would resemble a manuscript, Gutenberg had to deal with the work of two different craftsmen: the scribe and the illuminator. The work of the scribe was to copy out the text letter by letter in the particular style that was appropriate to the text he was transcribing; the work of the illuminator was to adorn the page of text with ornamental initials, paragraph marks, and other illustrations or illuminations. Gutenberg aimed in his discovery to supplant the work of the scribe; he saw no need to change the ancient and beautiful tradition of the illuminator. Accordingly, Gutenberg left blank spaces on his printed pages in which the illuminator could adorn the printed book exactly as he had been accustomed to adorn the manuscript book. Since each illuminator worked to his own designs and for a particular kind of client, the various copies of Gutenberg's great Bible are all decorated differently; no two are exactly alike. Fust and Schöffer, indeed, went one step further and reproduced with type even elaborate manuscript initials, but they soon discovered that such diligence, though remarkably successful, was more trouble than it was worth.

Though the hand illumination is commonly considered the more beautiful aspect of a page of one of Gutenberg's printed books, it is not the craft that concerns us here; our interest lies in the craft of the scribe—the making of letters.

may select among various styles of letter—elite, pica, IBM executive, italic, sans serif, etc.). The letter styles first copied were what we call *black letter,* the styles of lettering that were standard throughout all of Western Europe in the Middle Ages. These manuscript hands were five in number, four formal and one informal. (This distinction between formal and informal is still roughly preserved on official documents; at the bottom of such sheets we are likely to find two lines, on one of which appears the direction "Name (please print)" and on the other the direction "Signature" (i.e., please sign).

The four formal hands ("please print") were called *Textura, Fere-humanistica, Rotunda,* and *Bastarda.* The Textura, used chiefly for theological and liturgical works, was used in Gutenberg's Bible and in other of the earliest books (plate 14). It is defined by its strict angularity and freedom from curves (for example, the letter *o,* is made with six straight lines, the consequence of formal, i.e., slow, strokes of the quill. The Fere-humanistica had letters rounder and more open than those of the Textura and descenders ending bluntly without the feet of the Textura. It was used for general works in Latin. The Rotunda, used for vernacular works, is defined by the presence of curved letters within the straight formal lines of the Textura. The Bastarda, used for legal or general works, is the least formal in design, with many curved letters and with the "f" and long "s" descending below the line. The informal hand ("signature"), the cursive or casual handwriting of the period, was copied in a typeface that now seems rather florid. This face was cut first in the mid-sixteenth century, and though from its extravagance, it should have perished quickly, it nevertheless survived until the early nineteenth century. It was used until then as the standard face for the little manuals by which young hopefuls in France were to learn good manners or civility. Formerly called *French letter,* this face takes its modern name from such manuals—*Civilité.* It still appears occasionally as ornamental type for special effects.

The humanistic scribes of the early Renaissance felt that classical texts in Latin should be copied in a script that was classical—not in their "modern" black letter—and they chose as their model an elegant formal hand that they thought was from the classic period of Rome (modern scholarship has determined that the hand was Carolingian, not classical, in origin). Accordingly, the first printers in Italy, following this pattern, cut type designed after this (supposed) classical script to print their classical texts. They must have regarded it as a violent innovation. The first book printed in Italy, Cicero's *De oratore* (1465), was set in this deliberately antique form. It became the ancestor of all later *roman* faces. It was handsomely redesigned later by Nicholas Jenson and still further refined by the punch cutter

manifeſtū erit . Dies enim dñi declara
bit:qã ĩ igne reuelabit:ꝫ vniuſcuiuſꝗ
opus ꝗ̃le ſit ignis ꝓbabit . Bi cui⁹ o
pus māſerit qd̃ ſuꝑedificauit:mercede
accipiet.Bi cui⁹ op⁹ arſerit detrimētū
patiet̃:ipe aũt ſaluus erit:ſic tamē ꝗ̃ſi
ꝑ ignē. Aeſcitis qã tēplū dei eſtis:ꝫ ſpi
rit⁹ dei habitat ĩ vobis? Bi ꝗs autem
tēplū dei violauerit:diſpdet illū deus.
Tēplū eñi dei ſãctū ē̃: qd̃ eſtis vos. Ae
mo ſe ſeducat.Bi ꝗs videt̃ iter vos ſa
piēs eſſe ĩ hoc ſecd̃o:ſtul⁹ fiat ut ſit ſa
piēs.Bapiētia eñi hui⁹ mūdi ſtulticia
eſt apud deū.Bcriptū eſt eñi.Cōprehē
dam ſapientes in aſtutia eoꝫ . Et iterū.
De⁹ nouit cogitatõnes ſapiētiū : qñ
vane ſūt. Aemo itaꝗ glorietur in ho
minib3.Omnia eñi vr̃a ſūt:ſiue paul⁹
ſiue apollo ſiue cephas ſiue mund⁹
ſiue vita ſiue moꝛs ſiue ꝓſentia ſiue fu
tura . Omnia enim veſtra ſunt: vos
autem criſti:xp̃us autem dei. IIII

Bic nos exiſtimet homo ut mini
ſtros xp̃i:et diſpēſatores miſteri
oꝛ dei.Hic iã queritꝫ inter diſpēſatores:
ut fidelis ꝗs iueniatꝫ . Michi aũt ꝓ mi
nimo ē ut a vobis iudicet: aut ab hu
mano die . Bed neꝗ meipm̃ iudico.

Plate 14
Detail of Biblia (Mainz: Fust and Schöffer, ca. 1455). The Gutenberg Bible, 1 Cor.
3:13b–4:3 (Vulgate). Textura type. Compare with plates 5 and 28. (Courtesy of the
Folger Shakespeare Library.) (Slightly enlarged.)

Francesco Griffo, working for the famous printing house of Aldus Manutius in Venice. Griffo improved the tradition he received by returning to the marble inscriptions of imperial Rome for his models. The first book printed in France, Barzizius's *Epistolarum libri,* was printed at the Sorbonne in Roman letter in 1470. The informal script of the humanists, as used in the cursive handwriting of the papal chancery, was the model for the second "classical" typeface. Cut by Griffo for Aldus, this light letter, now called *italic* was first intended as a separate typeface to be used independently, and in it Aldus published his cheap and scholarly series of classical authors— not because it was beautiful, but because it was economical. However, thanks to the designer François Guyot, working for the house of Plantin in Antwerp, italic letter soon found its most appropriate function as the secondary and subordinate type in conjunction with roman, a position it still holds (as may be seen from the titles and the emphases in this paragraph).

The history of European type design is the history of the displacement of the Middle Ages by the Renaissance. Through the precedent set by Aldus in Italy and by the Sorbonne in France, the blackletter typefaces were gradually superseded by the "white-letter," or roman, type faces designed on classical models. The primacy of white letter was firmly established by about 1500, though works in the vernaculars continued for many years to appear in black letter. Indeed, modern descendants of black letter flourished in Germany, the last country to use black letter as the national standard, until 1941, when Adolf Hitler decreed that the face was Jewish in origin and not fit for the nation that was destined to rule the world. The face still has some currency on a small scale in the Netherlands for the printing of Bibles, and in America for special effects and for the printing of names of churches and newspapers.

Stanley Morison, the eminent historian of typography, has well described the transfer from black letter to white letter:

> Those who led the Renaissance forward [recognized that the roman letter] was a more efficient tool for the expression of their thought than either the text, pointed or rounded, or the vernacular cursive [i.e., the black-letter forms]; all these scripts they stigmatised as "Gothic." [That word meant to them something close to "barbarian," yet it is the word that has stuck as a name for the black-letter faces.] We know today that these pointed and rounded texts are perhaps the most homogeneous and beautiful scripts that have ever been evolved. No judge of the beauty of calligraphy [or type design] would prefer the slightly-built Roman to the full-bodied Gothic; yet the Roman . . . is in possession by right of conquest. . . . The victory of the Roman letter was due to its

**Plate 15**

Specimen sheet of types designed by François Guyot in Antwerp, ca. 1565. Since the marginal notes are written in the English "secretary" hand, computing the prices in pounds, shillings, and pence, it is assumed that the sheet was used in England as a guide to purchasing type from the continental foundry. (Courtesy of the Folger Shakespeare Library.) (Greatly reduced.)

inherent flexibility and rationalism . . . [and] to its power of adaptation to the infinite uses of modern work.*

In the fifteenth century—as now—type designers and casters prepared printed sheets displaying specimens of their various types, derived from the designs of the various scribal hands, and circulated them to printers who might wish to buy a *font* of type, i.e., a supply

---

*Stanley Morison, Introduction to *The New Hebrew Typography*, by Hugh J. Schonfield (London: Denis Archer, 1932), pp. 13, 12.

of all the different pieces of type for a single design and size. A glance at two of the earliest of such *specimen* sheets demonstrates precisely the transition indicated above. The earliest extant specimen dating from 1486 is that of Erhardt Ratdolt from Augsburg. It displays black-letter types of several designs and of ten different sizes and roman types of three sizes as well as type for Greek; the *Specimen Characterum* published by Plantin in 1567—eighty years later—displays black-letter types of six designs and sizes, roman of thirteen, and italic of eleven, as well as types for Greek, Hebrew, and Syriac. The oldest specimen sheet with specific English associations dates from about 1565 (plate 15); the specimen includes no black-letter fonts. The specimen was prepared by the designer François Guyot in Antwerp, but the marginal notations show that the sheet was used in England. Some three years after the date of this sheet, Guyot moved from Antwerp to London, where until his death in 1570 he cast for the Elizabethan printer John Day. It it probable that the popularity in England of the types exhibited on this specimen can be attributed to the influence of Guyot and his son.

The first type on the sheet, and the largest, Canon roman, appears in the headings of such large and important volumes as the King James Bible of 1611 and the Shakespeare First Folio of 1623. The next type is Double Pica, in roman and italic in both columns below the Canon roman. The two faces are evidently displayed here with the intention that they should be used in complementary fashion. The type in the lower left-hand column is Great Primer italic, used in the 1550s by Richard Tottell, the printer of the famous *Miscellany* (1558). (The specimen lacks a Great Primer roman, but Guyot had such a size, for it has been found in use in England from 1570 to 1662.) The smallest types, of the size used in most of the original editions of Shakespeare's single plays, are the Pica roman and italic.

## The Alphabet (A Digression)

The preceding paragraphs have assumed that the letters that Gutenberg was using were those of the Latin alphabet, and indeed possesion of that alphabet was one of the minor advantages that Gutenberg enjoyed in preparing his types. Theoretically, Gutenberg could have provided types for the single letters of the alphabet only (as on the modern typewriter); but as his originals, the scribal documents of the period, used a considerable number of abbreviations, contractions, and ligatures of these few letters, Gutenberg, in order to emulate these characteristic forms, cut nearly three hundred dif-

ferent sorts of letters and combinations of letters for his typecases.*
From that figure, the number of different sorts in a printer's cases
has steadily decreased, as type designers realized that they did not
have to copy the shapes of manuscript combinations and that movable type had an integrity of its own. During Shakespeare's time, a
few of these forms were still in use: one contraction, marked by the
"tilde" (or "tittle"), over a vowel to indicate the dropping of an *m* or
an *n* ("mā" to be read *man*; "cōmon" to be read *common*); ligatures
made with "f"—"fi" and "fl," "ff," "ffi" and "ffl"—and a parallel
system made with the long "s"; and the character "y" a type form of
scribal "th" from which we have unfortunately inherited "ye olde tea
shoppe" (plate 15 shows some of these forms). From this rich diversity of the abbreviations only the ampersand, "&," remains, preserved also in the informal writing of most of us; of the contractions
none remains; and of the ligatures, only those formed with "f"
remain (the long "s" began to disappear in English after 1785), and
in some few fonts a few others, such as "st" and "ct."

A few other changes have occurred in the printing alphabet as it
has descended from Gutenberg's time. We owe them to the Italian
poet Trissino, a spelling reformer, who in 1524 required that his
printer, Arrighi, make certain innovations. Before that date, the
characters "u" and "v" were both used to represent the letters *u* and
*v*, the character "u" representing them within the word, the character "v" representing them in initial position. Arrighi introduced the
distinction we now follow, though in Shakespeare's time *vpon* and
*loue* were still the standard printed forms. Arrighi followed Trissino
in using the character "j" to distinguish between the consonantal and
the vocalic functions of *i*. Trissino also used the Greek omega ω in his
poems, and it is from this that the modern double-u, or, as the
French say, "double-v," *w*, derives.

Though the Latin Alphabet was versatile, it did not represent
every language. The needs of expanding knowledge and commerce,
soon rendered the Latin alphabet insufficient. In the years 1465 to
1471 the Greek alphabet was cast on type, and not long after, in
1475, the Hebrew alphabet. Then followed Arabic and Russian,
and, for use chiefly in the universities, Syriac, Ethiopian, Samaritan,
and such other exotics as Anglo-Saxon (plate 16); in 1567, Queen
Elizabeth ordered that a font be cast for the Gaelic alphabet (plate

---

*Samples of these different sorts and combinations may be seen in plate 14 and (in English)
in Caxton's types in plate 24. In the Caxton there are two different forms of the letter "s" in
the first line *(so, dayes);* two different forms of the letter "r" in the second line *(were, for);* two
different forms of the letters "m" and "n" in the fifth line *(named, cam in);* combinations into
one sort in line four of "t" and "e" and of "d" and "e" *(wente, lande)* and of "r" and "e," "h" and
"e," "t" and "h" *(refreshe, them).*

Ælƿreðer æþ

Ic ða Ælƿreð cyning þær togædeɲ gegaðeɲoð.
Ᵹ aƿɲitan het. monega ðaɲa ðe uɲe ꝼoɲegengan
heolðon. ða þe me licoðon. Ᵹ ða ðe me ne licoðon ic
aƿeaɲƿ mið minɲa ƿitena geþeahte. Ᵹ on oþɲe ƿiɲan
bebeað to heolðáne; ꝼoɲþam ic ne ðuɲɲt geðyɲt-
læcan þæɲa minɲa apuht ꝼeala on geƿɲita ɲettan;
ꝼoɲþan me þær uncuþ hƿæt þær þæm lician polðe ðe
æꝼteɲ uɲ ƿæɲen; Ac þa þe ic gemette ahƿæɲ oþþe on
Ineɲ ðæge mineɲ mægeɲ. oþþe on Oꝼꝼá myɲcna cy-
ningeɲ. oþþe on Æþelbyɲhteɲ. þe æɲeɲt ꝼulƿiht un-
ðeɲꝼeng on angelcynne. ða þe me ɲihtoɲt þuhton.
ic þa heɲon gegaðeɲoð. Ᵹ þa oþɲe ꝼoɲlæte; Ic ða
Ælƿreð ƿeɲtɲeaxna cyning eallû minû ƿitum
þær geeoƿðe. Ᵹ hi þa cƿæðon. þ̅ him þ̅ lico-
ðe eallum to healðenne;

Be aþum. Ᵹ be peðlum;

Cap. ɪ.
Sonat etiã
peð. fidem
datam.

Æt æɲeɲtan ƿe læɲaþ. þ̅ mæɲt þeaɲꝼ iɲ. þ̅ æg-
hƿylce mon hiɲ áþ. Ᵹ hiɲ peð ƿæɲlic healðe;
Giꝼ hƿa to hƿæþeɲum þiɲɲum genyð ɲy on
ꝼoh. oþþe to hlaꝼoɲðe ɲyɲpe. oþþe to ænigum un-
ɲihtum ꝼultume. þ̅ iɲ þonne ɲihtɲe to aleogaɲne.
ðonne to gelæɲtanne; Giꝼ he ðonne ðær peððige
ðe

Plate 16
Text from William Lambard, *Archaionomia sive de priscis anglorum legibus libri* (London: John Day, 1568) (Anglo-Saxon and Latin). (Courtesy of the Folger Shakespeare Library.)

## The Communion.

OUr Father, which art in Heaven; Hallowed be thy Name. Thy Kingdom come. Thy will be done in Earth, As it is in Heaven. Give us this day our daily bread. And forgive us our trespasses, As we forgive them that trespass against us. And lead us not into temptation ; But deliver us from evil : For thine is the kingdom, the power, and the glory, For ever and ever. Amen.

*¶ After shall be said as followeth.*

OLord, and heavenly Father, we thy humble servants entirely desire thy Fatherly goodness, mercifully to accept this our sacrifice of praise and thanksgiving ; most humbly beseeching thee to grant, that by the merits and death of thy Son Jesus Christ, and through faith in his blood, we and all thy whole Church may obtain remission of our sins, and all other benefits of his passion. And here we offer and present unto thee, O Lord, our selves, our souls and bodies, to be a reasonable, holy, and lively sacrifice unto thee ; humbly beseeching thee, that all we who are partakers of this holy Communion, may be fulfilled with thy grace and heavenly benediction. And although we be unworthy through our manifold sins to offer unto thee any sacrifice ; yet we beseech thee to accept this our bounden duty and service ; not weighing our merits, but pardoning

## An Chomaoin

AR Natg, a tá ap ngím ; ncómtap hainm. Tiggð ðo piogap. Ðíntap ðo toil ap talam, map nítiop ap ngím. Tabg ðpñ a niuð ap napán lætceampl. Aguy mait ðpñ ap acionta, map maitmiðne ðáib ðo ciontaiggy ap nagaið. Aguy na tpéopaið iñ cum eataigte ; at pðp iñ óolc : óip ay let an piogap, 7 an cumay, 7 an gloip, go bpát 7 go bpát. Amen.

*¶ An sin deartbar mar Leanas.*

OA tiggpna, 7 Atg ngímða, tá pñe ðo peipbpið umla go ðúbpapac ag gpðe ðo maitgpa acapða, ap móbðgtge mólaið, 7 tabapta bpðgcaiy ðo gabáil go tpócðgge ; go po umal ðoð gpðe, cñtaðð go bpñgenne 7 heglaip ple, tpñ luaiðgp 7 bay lópa Cpíoyð, 7 tpñ cpeiðgm añ a pñl, maitgín-nay ap bpgcaiðe, 7 gac ple thaipbhe eile a phaipipion. Agay añ po, a tiggpna, toimbip-mið iñ péin, ap nanmana 7 ap gcoipp, cum a mbeit na mioð-bðc péapúnta, ncómta, 7 béoða ðptyi ; ðoð gpðe go humal go mbeitmipne ple, tá pappðgtg ya comóin naoimtaya, liónta lé ðo gpáya 7 lé ðo bgnaða ngimðaya. Agay ap pon nach piuð pñ tpñ ap moliomað pg-caiðe ioðbðt ap bit ðo toim-bipt ðpt ; Bíðgð gpómið tú an ðualgay 7 a tyeipbipe tá ðpiðcaið opaiñ, ðo gabáil ; ni ag mgðacan ap luaiðgpne, ap our

ᎣᏍᏛ ᎧᏃᎮᏛ, ᎷᎦ ᎤᏬᏪᎳᏅᎯ.

ᎠᏯᏙᎸᎢ I.

1 ᎾᏍᎩᏃ ᎠᏂᎪᏗᏳ ᏧᎾᏁᎶᏔᏅ Ꭼ-
ᏂᎨᏒ ᎢᏳᏅᏁᏗᏱ ᎧᏃᎲᏍᎩ ᏧᏓᎴᏅᏛ
ᏄᎵᏍᏔᏂᏙᎸ ᎾᏍᎩ ᎤᏙᎯᏳᎯᏯ ᏦᎪ-
ᎯᏳᎭ,
2 ᎾᏍᎩᏯ ᏂᎪᎩᏪᏎᎸ ᎾᏍᎩ ᏗᏓᎴ-
ᏂᏍᎬ ᏅᏓᎬᏩᏓᎴᏅᏛ ᎤᏅᏒ ᎤᏂᎪᎯ-
ᏙᎸᎯ, ᎠᎴ ᎧᏃᎮᏛ ᎤᎾᎵᏥᏙᏅᎯ Ꭸ-
ᏒᎢ—
3 ᎾᏍᏉ ᎠᏴ ᎣᏏᏳ ᎠᎩᏰᎸᏅ ᏫᎬ-
ᏲᏪᎳᏁᏗᏱ ᎣᏍᏛ ᎠᎩᏰᎢᏎᏍᏗᏱ,
ᏂᎯ ᎡᏣᎸᏉᏗ ᏗᎣᏈᎵ, ᎠᎩᏍᏆᏂᏰᏛ-
ᏰᏃ ᏂᎦᏛ ᎯᎠ ᏧᏓᎴᏅᏛ ᏗᏓᎴᏂᏍᎬ
ᏅᏓᎬᏩᏓᎴᏅᏛ,
4 ᎾᏍᎩ ᏣᎦᏙᎥᎯᏍᏗᏱ ᎤᏙᎯᏳᎯᏯ
ᎨᏒ ᎾᏍᎩ ᎾᎿ ᏧᏓᎴᏅᏛ ᎡᏤᏲᏅᎢ.
5 ᎾᎯᏳ ᎡᎶᏛ ᎤᎬᏫᏳᎯ ᎨᏎ Ꮷ-
ᏗᏱ, ᎩᎶ ᎢᏳᏍᏗ ᎡᎮ ᎠᏥᎸ-ᎨᎶᎯ
ᏤᎦᎳᏯ ᏧᏙᎢᏛ, ᎾᏍᎩ ᎡᏆᏯ ᎠᎦᏘ-
ᏅᏔᏅ ᎨᎳ ᎨᏎᎢ, ᎤᏓᎵᎢᏃ ᎡᎳᏂ
ᏧᏪᏥᏛᎯ ᎨᏒ ᏅᏓᏳᏓᎴᏅᎯ ᎨᏎᎢ,
ᎠᎴ ᎵᏏ ᏚᏙᎡᎢ.
6 ᎠᎴ ᎢᏧᎳ ᏚᏳᎪᏛ ᏧᏂᎸᏫᏍᏓᏁᎯ
ᎨᏎ ᎤᏁᎳᏅᎯ ᏙᏗᎧᏅᎢ, ᏓᏂᎧᎿᏩ-
ᏗᏎ ᏂᎦᏛ ᏗᎧᎿᏩᏛᏍᏗ ᎠᎴ ᎤᎵᏁᏨ
ᎢᏯᏛᏁᎵᏓᏍᏗ ᎨᏒ ᏱᎰᏩ ᏧᏤᎵᎦ,
ᎤᏲᏅ ᏂᎨᏥᎳᎾᏎᎲᎾ.
7 ᎠᎴ ᏁᎲᎾ ᎨᏎ ᎤᏁᏥ, ᎵᏏᏰᏃ
ᎥᏝ ᏱᏓᎷᎸᎥᏍᎨᎢ, ᎠᎴ ᎢᏧᎳ ᎿᏉ Ꭰ-
ᏂᎦᏴᎵᎨ ᎨᏎᎢ.
8 ᎯᎠᏃ ᏄᎵᏍᏔᏁᎢ, ᎾᏍᎩ ᎠᏥᎸ-
ᎨᎶᎯ ᏧᎸᏫᏍᏓᏁᏗ ᎨᏒ ᏕᎸᏫᏍᏓᏁᎮ
ᎤᏁᎳᏅᎯ ᎠᎦᏔᎲᎢ, ᎾᎯᏳ ᎤᎵᏱᎶᎸ
ᏧᏂᎸᏫᏍᏓᏁᏗᏱ ᎾᎿ ᎨᎸᎢ,
9 ᎾᏍᎩ ᎢᏳᎾᏛᏁᏗ ᎨᏒ ᎠᏥᎸ-
ᎠᏁᎶᎯ, ᎾᏍᎩ ᎤᏩᏙᏗ ᏂᎦᎵᏍᏗᏍᎨ
ᎠᏜ ᎦᏩᏒᎩ ᎾᎯᏳ ᏩᏴᎭ ᏱᎰᏩ ᎤᏤᎵ
ᎤᏛᏅ-ᏗᎦᎳᏫᎢᏍᏗᏱ.
10 ᎤᏂᏣᏘᏃ ᏴᏫ ᏙᏱᏗᏢ ᎠᎾᏓᏙᎵ-
ᏍᏗᏍᎨ ᎾᎯᏳ ᎠᏜ ᎦᏩᏒᎩ ᎬᏙᏗᏱ
ᎤᏍᏆᎸᎲ.
11 ᏱᎰᏩᏃ ᎤᏤᎵ ᏗᎧᎿᏩᏗᏙᎯ ᎬᏂ-
ᎨᏒ ᏄᏛᏁᎴ ᎦᏙᎨ ᎠᎦᏘᏏᏗᏢ ᎦᏩᏒᎩ
ᎬᏙᏗᏱ ᎪᏢᏒᎢ.
12 ᏤᎦᎳᏯᏃ ᎤᎪᎲ, ᎤᏕᏯᏔᏁᎴ
ᎠᎴ ᎤᏍᎦᎴᎢ.
13 ᎠᏎᏃ ᏗᎧᎿᏩᏗᏙᎯ ᎯᎠ ᏄᏪᏎ-
ᎴᎢ; ᏤᎦᎳᏯ ᏞᏍᏗ ᏣᏍᎦᎸᎩ; ᎭᏓ-
ᏙᎵᏍᏗᏍᎬᏰᏃ ᎡᏣᏛᎦᏁᎸ; ᎠᎴ ᏣᏓ-
ᎵᎢ ᎵᏏ ᏓᏣᎾᏄᎪᏫᏎᎵ ᏤᏥ ᎠᏧᏣ, Ꮳ-
ᏂᏃ ᏕᎯᏲᎥᎭ.
14 ᎠᎴ ᎭᎵᎮᎵᎨᏍᏗ ᎠᎴ ᎣᏍᏛ
ᏣᏰᎸᏎᏍᏗ; ᎠᎴ ᎤᏂᏣᏘ ᎠᎾᎵᎮᎵᎨ-
ᏍᏗ ᎤᏕᏅ ᎢᏳᏍᏗ.
15 ᎠᎴ ᎠᏥᎸᏉᏗᏳ ᎨᏎᏍᏗ Ᏹ-
ᎰᏩ ᏙᏗᎧᏅᎢ, ᎥᏝ ᎠᎴ ᎤᏗᏔᏍᏗ ᏱᎨ-
ᏎᏍᏗ ᎩᎦᎨ-ᎠᏗᏔᏍᏗ ᎠᎴ ᎠᏓᏴᏍᏕ-
ᏍᏗᏍᎩ; ᎠᎴ ᎤᎧᎵᏨᎯ ᎨᏎᏍᏗ Ꮥ-
ᎸᏉᏗᏳ ᎠᏓᏅᏙ, ᎤᏥ ᎤᎾᏄᎪᏫᏒ
ᏅᏓᎬᏩᏓᎴᏅᏛ.
16 ᎠᎴ ᎤᏂᏣᏘ ᎢᏏᎵ ᏧᏪᏥ ᏙᏛᎪ-
ᎸᏏ ᏱᎰᏩ ᎤᎾᏁᎳᏅᎯ ᎢᏗᏢ ᏙᏛᎦ-
ᎳᎲᏍᏔᏂ.
17 ᎠᎴ ᎢᎬᏱ ᏓᏳᏪᏅᏒᎵ [ᎤᎬᏫ-
ᏳᎯ] ᎢᎳᏯ ᎾᏍᎩᏯ ᎨᏎᏍᏗ ᎤᏓᏅ-
ᏙᎩ ᎠᎴ ᎤᎵᏂᎩᏗᏳ ᎨᏒᎢ, ᏗᎦᎳᎲ-
ᏍᏗᏱ ᏧᏂᏙᏓ ᎠᏂᎦᏴᎵᎨᎢ ᏗᏂᏲᎵ Ꭲ-
ᏗᏢ ᏫᏚᎦᏔᎲᏍᏙᏗᏱ, ᎠᎴ ᏄᏃᎯᏳᏒᎾ
ᏗᎦᏔᎲᏍᏗᏱ ᎤᎾᏓᏅᏘ ᎠᏂᎦᏔᎿᎥ ᎢᏗᏢ

LUKE

Plate 18
Text from the Holy Bible (New York: American Bible Society, 1860). Luke 1 : 1–17 (Cherokee Indian). (Reproduced from the copy in the Department of Rare Books, Perkins Library, Duke University, Durham, North Carolina, with kind permission.)

17). When the Bible was first translated into an American Indian language in 1650, it was printed phonetically in the Latin alphabet. Not until the nineteenth century did an Indian language receive its own written "alphabet"—the syllabary devised by Sequoyah for the Cherokee Nation in Georgia. Type was cut for this alphabet and a newspaper was first printed in it in 1828; the New Testament was printed in 1860 (plate 18). But this brave effort was doomed to extinction. Though the language is still preserved by native speakers in North Carolina and Oklahoma, the alphabet is maintained only as a historical curiosity.

There are some signs now that the Latin alphabet may eventually become the printing alphabet of the world (though it is not well suited for some language families). In 1928 the Turkish government abandoned the Arabic character in favor of the Latin to represent the Turkic language, in 1958 the Chinese State Council began the slow process of replacing the Chinese ideograph with the Latin letter, and now in Lebanon a small group of speakers of Arabic have adopted the Latin letter for the Arabic language. On the other hand, the Irish, after securing independence from Britain in 1921, reverted officially to the use of the Irish language in the Gaelic character. A sign "of the deep cleavage between East and West," as a modern historian has pointed out, is the retention of the Cyrillic letter in the Soviet Union.

---

*Cutting and Casting the Letter.* When he had decided the designs of the letters that he wished to reproduce in type, Gutenberg then had the task of cutting or engraving these designs on steel punches from which to make the actual pieces of type. This task was simplicity itself, for as a goldsmith Gutenberg would regularly have cut letters on just such punches in order to strike inscriptions or his own hallmark on metal objects of many kinds. The letter design, once engraved *(positive)*, was then used to strike an impression *(negative)* in a softer metal, usually an alloy of copper, called a *matrix*.

Though the designing and cutting of these earliest types presented few problems, their casting or founding required the greatest ingenuity. The success of the entire activity depended primarily on two inventions: the mold and the alloy.

The mold was a box of wood and steel, held in the hand, a device to form the pieces of type for printing. It provided a little rectangular receptacle (or *channel*), the bottom of which was the matrix with the letter stamped in it. The depth of the receptacle *(height to paper)* was fixed by the size of the mold for the font desired, and this was standardized eventually so that all pieces of type from all molds would stand at exactly the same level when put upright on the bed of the press. The dimensions of the flat area of the bottom of the mold (the *face*) depended on (1) the height and (2) the width of the particular letter.

The height of the letter—i.e., the distance between the top and bottom of the capital letter, "M" or "I," for example—determined the choice of the size of mold. For each of the different sizes of type—as shown in plate 15—there was a corresponding size of mold. For each size of type, of course, the capital letters printed on the page would have more height than the small letters; but all the letters of a given size, of the font, would be cast on blocks of the same height so that all the pieces of type from a particular mold would form parallel lines of text when set in a sequence side by side and one above the other. While the height of the letters of a given size was uniform, the width of the letters was variable, and therefore the mold was made adjustable so as to widen or diminish to accommodate "M" or "I," for example. Gutenberg might have simplified his technique by using the same width for every letter—as some standard typewriters still do, squeezing "M" into the space suitable for "I"; but again Gutenberg followed the patterns of the manuscripts that he sought to emulate. Some historians consider the mechanism that allowed the mold to be adjusted to the widths of the various letters the most important single unit of all of Gutenberg's inventions.

To produce pieces of type, the caster placed in his mold the matrix for a letter, poured into the receptacle the molten type metal, and then agitated the mold so that the metal would fill the design of the cut letter properly. When the metal cooled, he opened the mold, ejected the type, and smoothed off its rough edges (plate 19).

The modern typewriter manages well with one piece of "type" for each letter of the alphabet, but it is evident that to print a page of text requires many more than one sample of each letter; it requires *multiple* copies. To produce the preceding sentence will require twenty-nine individual samples, or "sorts," of the letter "e," nineteen of the letter "t," three of the letter "w," one of the letter "x," and one of the capital "T"; furthermore, it will require one of "*e*," one of "*t*," and two of "*l*." Gutenberg had to provide types that were not only movable, interchangeable, and reusable—but available in quantity. He devised the mold, therefore, so that it could be a device for mass production. The skillful type caster did, and still can, produce with his hand mold some four thousand pieces of type in one day.

The first printers included typecasting as one of their normal operations, and the Scoloker woodcut of 1548 (plate 11) shows in the background a typecaster working in the shop; but before the

## Fuſor literarıus. Der Schrifftgieſſer.

*CAlcographis fundens ex ære fideliter omnes*
*Literulas, conflo quaslibet arte notas.*
*Siue Latina meum, ſeu Gallica lingua requirit*
*Officium, Doctis pareo ſponte viris.*

*Ipſa mei paßim quoq Græcia muneris arte*
*Indiget, egregios cùm premit ære libros.*
*Hæc foret ars noſtra niſi tempeſtate reperta,*
*Nunc mihi ſcribarum functio quanta foret?*
*Plura breuis ſpacio quia ſcripta Typographus horæ*
*Edit, quam multis ſcriba diebus agat.*

Adum⸗

Plate 19
Woodcut, "Typefounder," from *Panoplia* (Frankfurt: Hartman Schopperum, 1568).
(Courtesy of the Folger Shakespeare Library.)

printing industry was a decade old, the function of designing and casting types was growing into a specialized trade, and by 1600 almost all of the founding was accomplished in three great type foundries: Guyot-Plantin (Antwerp), Egenolff (Frankfurt), and Le Bé (Paris).

The identification of the alloy to be used as the type metal presented a serious problem, and Gutenberg's solution to it constitutes another of his major discoveries. Gutenberg discovered that a formula of lead, tin, and iron (soon replaced by antimony) would heat easily and cool quickly, would readily fill the design of the letter in the matrix, and would retain this figure over a long period of use.

Most important of all, the alloy would not expand or shrink in the process of heating and cooling. This formula must have consisted of approximately 75 percent lead, 12 percent tin, 12 percent antimony, and 1 percent copper. The discovery of these particular proportions is, in essence, the heart of Gutenberg's achievement in creating the alloy, for it made possible the proper fusion of the tin and the antimony. (Formulas now in use reduce the amount of lead and increase the amounts of the other ingredients, but modern type-casters are still, in general terms, following Gutenberg's formula.)

## The Ink

The perfection of a printing ink was another of Gutenberg's in-genious works. In the fourteenth and early fifteenth centuries, scribes and printers of wood blocks used a light, water-based ink (roughly comparable to the ink for modern fountain pens). This kind of ink, though satisfactory for wood and for manuscript, tends to separate into individual droplets when placed on metal, and Gutenberg must have recognized early in his experiments that it would not serve for his new types. He found the answer to the problem in oil, similar to the oil of the colors of the Flemish painters (notably Jan Van Eyck, who died in 1441, just as Gutenberg was achieving the successful end of his project). Gutenberg developed an oil-based fluid of high viscosity (roughly comparable to the ink for modern ball-point pens), ideal for his purposes, that would stick evenly to the types as they stood on the flatbed and, when pressure was applied, would adhere only to the paper immediately pressed by the type without "bleeding," leaking, or staining adjoining fibers. Furthermore, the inks were, as we can still observe today, exception-ally brilliant and solidly black. Recent analysis by electron particles has demonstrated that that denseness also derives from the Flemish painters' oil paints, for like those oils, Gutenberg's inks had high metallic content: small amounts of titanium, large amounts of lead and copper. The uniqueness of Gutenberg's inks appears from a comparison with the oldest surviving formula for printer's ink. This recipe, dating from 1617, requires only juniper gum, linseed oil, and lampblack. Gutenberg did not stint; later printers and inkmak-ers, motivated by attempts at economy, did not maintain the high excellence of Gutenberg's ink. In addition to this strong black, Gutenberg had also a red ink for rubrics and capitals, and Fust and Schöffer had a blue.

In the process of printing, the semisolid ink was scooped out of the jar that contained it and placed on an ink tray or ink block beside the press. From this block the pressman transfered the ink by means of two ink balls held in his hands. He picked up ink from the block on the balls by rocking them over the ink in a rotary motion. He then transferred the ink from the balls to the type with the same motion. While awaiting the return of the type from the press, he rotated the balls together in order to assure an even distribution of the ink on them. He replenished the supply of ink on the balls after two or three impressions, though pages of densely set type might require a fresh supply after each impression. He regularly examined the printed sheets to discover whether he was inking sufficiently or not. Plate 11 shows the apprentice waiting while the impression is being taken; he holds the two ink balls together, distributing the ink on them. Plate 12 shows one pressman engaged in inking the type.

When two men of equal experience worked a press, it was the custom to alternate shifts, the task of inking being less strenuous than that of pulling the heavy bar and moving the types. The task of inking, on the other hand, was often assigned to a young apprentice.

Ink balls, about six to seven inches in diameter, were made of wool or horsehair covered with leather fastened to a wooden handle. At the end of each day's work, the balls were disassembled. The wool stuffing was cleaned, and the leather casing was soaked in urine. The odors must have been remarkable.

Another fluid of the printing operation appears in the 1581 woodcut of the London press (plate 12). That cut shows, in a prominent place, a flagon; as this feature does not appear in the Dutch original of which this is a copy or in illustrations of printing shops from other nations, it must be regarded as a device for refreshment peculiar to the English temperament.

## The Paper

The surfaces that were available to Gutenberg and suitable to receive printing inks were two: vellum (or parchment) and paper. Gutenberg, still following the example of the scribes, used both, printing some of the copies of the forty-two line Bible on vellum. Vellum, though serviceable, was expensive, and Gutenberg must have imagined that a copy of his Bible printed on vellum, could— like an elegant manuscript—constitute a "luxury item." But Gutenberg must soon also have recognized that the luxury trade was already well supplied by the producers of manuscripts and that there was no need to serve that market and no special appropriateness in attempting to do so. The function of the printing press in all its marvellous fecundity was to communicate texts to a wide and numerous reading public, not to a select few. That mass market could not be served by the supply of vellum, which was manifestly limited; that market required paper, the supply of which must have seemed inexhaustible. Furthermore, there was probably little profit to be gained from printing on vellum. A book printed on vellum in the fifteenth century sold at three times the cost of the same volume printed on paper; one hundred years later, when the manuscript tradition had all but died out, and, we may suppose, the production of vellum for the trade was going the same way, a book printed on vellum sold at eight times the cost of the volume on paper. Though these prices may seem to represent a substantial increase in income, it should be remembered that there would be few such books, that the printing stock would be expensive, and that the individual attention required for each one would be time-consuming. Gutenberg, the first modern mass-media expert, realized that the future lay with paper.

Papermaking had come from the East in the twelfth century, and the manufacture of paper soon became an industry widespread over continental Europe, wherever a stream provided power for a mill. Paper was made from old rags, preferably linen, which, after being washed, were set aside for several days to rot. Then they were cut into small pieces and pounded by water-driven hammers into pulp called *stuff.* The pulp was then placed in a large open vat over a low fire and stirred. When the stuff had reached the proper consistency, the papermaker dipped a rectangular papermold into the vat, scooping up a supply of the pulp on the mold (see plate 20). The papermold consisted of a wooden frame over which were stretched as a grid heavy wires (called *chains*), parallel to the short side of the frame and about one inch apart, and light wires (called *wires*) laid over the heavy wires, parallel to the long side of the frame and about one millimeter apart. The wire grid of the mold acted as a sieve. As the water drained through, the papermaker shook the mold sideways, thereby joining together the fibers in the pulp and creating (or *shutting*) the one individual sheet. When the sheets of pulp had gained solidity, they were laid on rectangular felt pads in a pile and placed in a press where the excess moisture was squeezed out. After this process had made each sheet a recognizable unit of paper, the felt intersheets were removed and the paper was pressed again. Then the sheets were dried and packaged for sale. Paper made by this sheet-by-sheet process can be detected by holding a sheet up to the light: examination reveals at once the impressions left in the paper by the chains and by the wires; plate 21 shows the lines clearly.

Plate 21 shows also an identifying mark, or *watermark,* the impression left in the paper by a wire device fastened to the papermarker's

## Chartarius. Der Papyrer.

*EX vetulis pannis tenuem contexo papyrum,*
*Vertitur in gyros dum mola scabra suos:*
*In tabulis olim sua scripsit verba vetustas,*
*Quas rudis ex cæra dextra liquente dabat.*

*Cùm mera simplicitas æuo rarißima nostro,*
*Et merus in terris scribere iußit amor.*
*Principibus nostris vix sufficit aurea charta,*
*Sit licet aurata sæpe notata manu.*
*Fama vetus nulli certos adscripsit honores,*
*Istius inuentor qui prior artis erat.*

C   4     Conci-

Plate 20
Woodcut, "Papermaker," from *Panoplia* (Frankfurt: Hartman Schopperum, 1568). (Courtesy of the Folger Shakespeare Library.)

mold. The watermark identifies the specific mold in which the paper was made and thus the specific paper mill. Marks often consisted of floral, animal, or heraldic devices or of initials or the numerals of the year. This watermark illustrated contains the initials "E R" surmounted by a crown. It identifies the paper as a sheet from a special stock prepared for Queen Elizabeth by the papermarker John (later Sir John) Spilman. In 1589 Spilman had been granted the patent to produce white paper; as the text written on this paper (a letter from

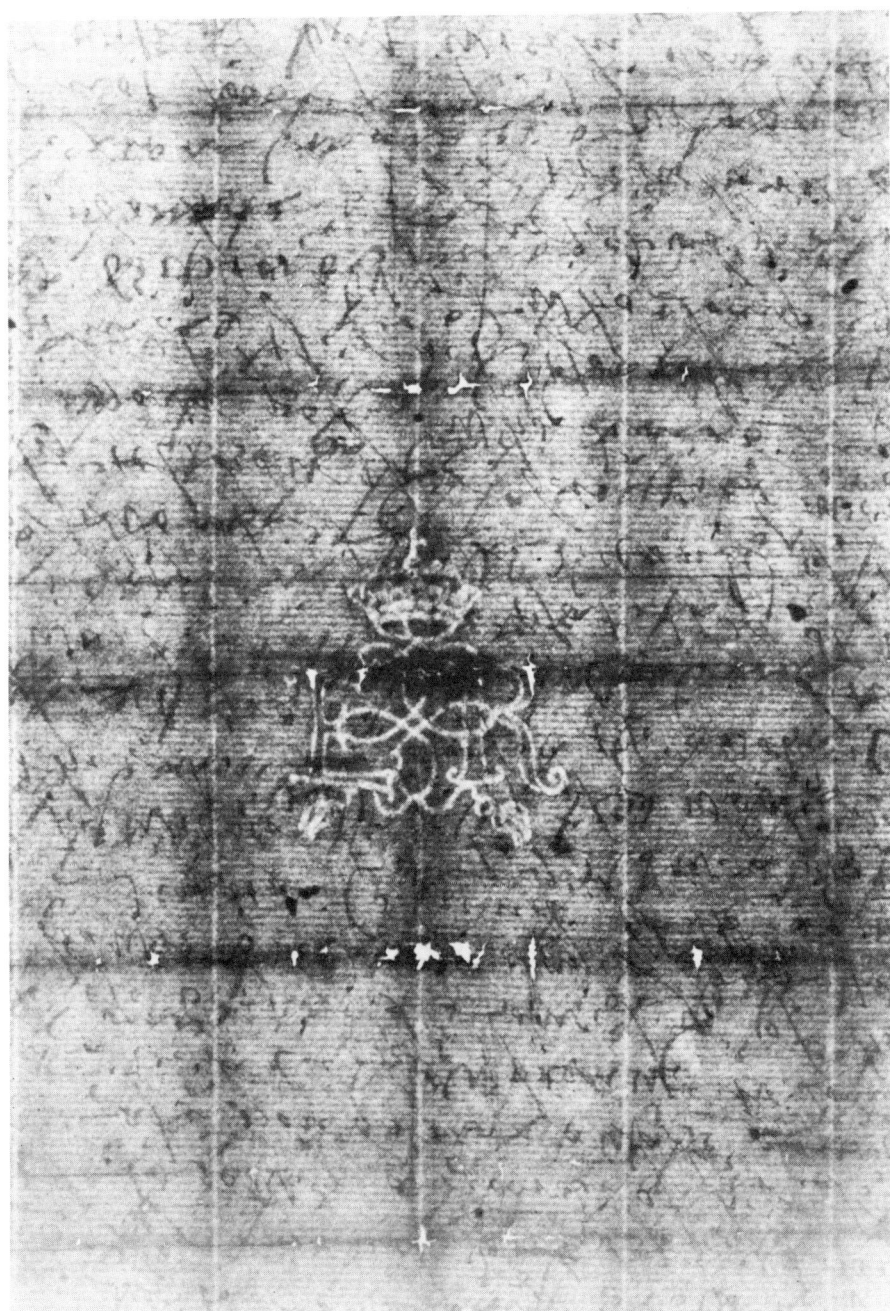

Plate 21

Detail of paper, showing chain lines (vertical), wire lines (horizontal), and watermark of the letters *E* and *R* surmounted by a crown. The watermark identifies the paper as from the stock made by John Spilman for Queen Elizabeth, 1589–93. (Courtesy of the Folger Shakespeare Library.)

Queen Elizabeth to James VI of Scotland) can be dated about 1593, the paper is evidently some of the first to be produced by Spilman's mill.

Watermarks can also be seen in printed books of the period, the location of the watermark on the pages of the bound volume varying with the various methods of folding the paper in making the book (as we shall see in the next section).

Papermaking developed slowly in England. In the fifteenth and sixteenth centuries several small mills were established, notably that of John Tate at Stevenage (1495–98), but these lasted only a short time and tended to manufacture chiefly brown paper rather than the white paper needed for writing and printing. The reason for this sluggishness was simply the excellence and cheapness of continental papers. It was easier to import than to manufacture. Though Spilman, the special patentee of the crown, was a successful papermaker, as a rule the products of English papermakers were unable to compete with foreign imports in cost or quality until the eighteenth century.

The size of a sheet of paper depended on the size of the mold in which it was made, and the maximum size of the mold depended on the size that a worker could handle. In the fourteenth and fifteenth centuries, four sizes of mold were generally agreed upon and standard in Western Europe, producing papers of these sizes: Imperial (75 × 50 cm.; 29″ × 19¾″), Royal (60 × 44cm.; 24″ × 17½″), Demy (i.e., one-half the Imperial: 50 × 35 cm.; 19½″ × 13¾″), Foolscap (45 × 31.5cm.; 17½″ × 12½″). In the sixteenth century two other sizes developed: Crown (between Demy and Foolscap), Pot (smaller than Foolscap); in the seventeenth century another size developed: Medium (between Royal and Demy). There was thus great variety available in sizes, which were never exactly measured and which depended much on the individual papermaker.

The size of the original sheet determined the size of all books made from it, since the original sheet could be treated so as to produce either one single large page or folded, each successive fold producing pages one-half the size of the one before it. The following terms describe the various sizes and foldings of the sheets.

1. *Broadside.* A sheet of paper laid on the type and printed to produce one page, one single block of type (on each side), without folding, is called a *broadside* or *broadsheet* (1° is the symbol for this size); such a piece of printed work is quite large, but it might be used as an advertisement or as an official notice to be posted up or, several such sheets collected and fastened together, for an atlas with large illustrations.

2. *Folio.* A sheet of paper laid on the type and printed to produce two pages, two separate blocks of type (two pages on each side of the paper), with one fold between them, is called a *folio* (2°), and a book composed of such sheets folded once, thus yielding two leaves, four pages, for each sheet, is similarly called. Plate 12 shows, on the press, a sheet that has been printed to be folded down the middle (with a fold parallel to the short side) in a folio.

3. *Quarto.* A sheet of paper laid on the type and printed to produce four pages, four separate blocks of type (four pages on each side) with two folds is called a *quarto* (4°), and a book composed of such sheets folded twice, thus yielding four leaves, eight pages, for each sheet, is similarly called.

4. *Octavo, etc.* The series continues with additional foldings to *octavo* ($8^{vo}$), folded thrice yielding eight leaves; to *sixteens* ($16^{mo}$), *thirty-twos* ($32^{mo}$), and *sixty-fours* ($64^{mo}$).

5. *Twelvemo, etc.* An intermediate system, popular because it yielded books more convenient for handling than did some of the preceding, resulted from different foldings and from cutting the sheets: *twelves* ($12^{mo}$), *eighteens* ($18^{mo}$), and *twenty-fours* ($24^{mo}$).

## *The Printing Process*

When a text was to be printed, the master printer or the bookseller or the publisher judged from the nature of the document, its length, and the number of copies likely to be bought by its supposed reading public, what the format, type size and design, and paper quality and quantity would be; and on the basis of such decisions he obtained sufficient supplies of suitable types and paper to execute the work. Depending on many factors, the work might be set up in a print shop by a single typesetter, or *compositor,* or by two or three or more working simultaneously, alternately, or consecutively (some eight compositors worked in a single shop to set up the Shakespeare First Folio in 1623); if there was need for haste, the work might be parceled out among several shops (five or more shops printed sections of the Beaumont and Fletcher Folio in 1647, the separate sections being brought together to be bound into a single volume). The critical figures in the entire process were the compositors, because it was through their minds and fingers that the ideas of the text before them were "committed to type." (Plates 3, 4, and 12 show compositors at their cases.)

Though compositors were, generally, faithful to their responsibility to the author, they answered also to another responsibility, a responsibility to the craft: to normalize and standardize the author's idiosyncratic spellings, forms, capitalization, and punctuation. In that process, however, they tended to reveal their own individual idiosyncratic standards, and it is often possible, by a close study of printed texts of the early period, to discover the particular typographical habits and spelling preferences of the compositor(s) who set up specific texts. Such studies, yielding information as to the kinds of errors an individual compositor is likely to make, guide modern editors in the preparation of editions. The most conspicuous successes in this kind of inquiry have been achieved in studies of Shakespeare's plays.

## Composition

When a text was to be printed, the typesetter, or compositor, was charged with the *composition* of the text into type. With the manuscript before him, the compositor set up the words of the text in type, letter by letter, taking type sorts from his two "cases" of type—capital letters *(majuscule)* from the upper case, small letters *(minuscule)* from the lower case. He placed the pieces of type (upside down) in a *composing stick* in his left hand so that they formed a line of type. If the line of type, as is likely in prose, was not exactly the length of the width of the column that had been chosen for the format of the book, he adjusted the types of his stick so that they were exactly that dimension. This *justification* he accomplished by the free and vigorous use of contractions when he was setting a text in Latin; when he was setting a text in English, which lacks a full system of scribal contractions, he justified his line by varying the spelling of the words (the lexicographers had not yet developed a fixed system of spelling for the English language) or by using blank spaces (in the setting of verse, the problem of justification was solved by the use of blank spaces). When the line was set in his stick, the compositor read it over for correctness of sense and neatness of typography and then proceeded to the next line, placing its types in the stick above those of the preceding line. When several lines had been so composed, the compositor transferred them to the *galley* and carried on. When the page of text was complete, the compositor added three guides that would be helpful later: (1) on the line below the text on each page he set the first word of the next page, the *catchword*—a device to assist him in keeping the pages in proper sequence when he arranged them in position for the actual printing by the press; (2) on a line below the catchword, on the first page of the sheet, he set in alphabetical sequence a letter for the sheet, the *signature**—a device to assist the binders in keeping the sheets in proper sequence when they were to be bound—and (3) on the first few right-hand pages of each sheet, he set beside the letter for the sheet a number for the leaf—a device to assist the binders in keeping the leaves in proper sequence when they were folding the sheets. Having finished a page with these guides, the compositor tied a bit of string about the lines of type and transferred this *type-block* to a flat table, the *imposing stone,* to take its place in the making up of the *forme,* i.e., all the material to be printed at one time.

The number of pages to be printed at one time depends on the format of the book to be printed. For a folio volume the printer will print two pages at one time on one side of the sheet and then will print two pages on the other side of the sheet (*perfect* the sheet). The pages that fill either side of the sheet constitute one forme. The pages that will lie on the inside of the sheet when it is folded constitute the *inner forme;* those on the outside, the *outer forme.* The pages of the inner forme of a sheet in folio will be pages two and three; the pages of the outer forme will be pages one and four. All of the pages of a forme are printed simultaneously.

If a compositor sets his copy straight through from beginning to end *(seriatim),* he will be obliged in folio printing, for example, to put page one aside and complete pages two and three before he can send anything to the press to be printed. When he has finished pages two and three and arranged them in the proper order, i.e., *imposed* them as the inner forme, he may send them to the press to print one side of the sheet while he continues with page four. When page four is completed, he imposes it with page one to constitute the outer forme and sends it to the press to perfect the sheet.

It will be evident that a page of type standing idly by wastes both time and type. Accordingly, to save both time and type, the compositor would often *cast off* his copy, computing in advance exactly how much of the text he would put on each page—i.e., where each page would end. Difficult as it may seem, the process of casting off

---

*The term *signature* refers first to the actual letter that designates the particular sheet; by metonomy, it refers also to the entire sheet or, when modified, to the particular leaf of the sheet or to the particular side of the leaf, i.e., page. In this pamphlet, it will refer only to the letter, as here. Though signatures are not found in most American books, some English printing houses still use them as the traditional, and still effective, way of keeping the sheets in proper sequence. If in setting a long book, the Renaissance compositor ran through the entire alphabet in signatures, he would begin a second alphabet consisting of doubled letters or of letters of a different font. The signatures of the Shakespeare First Folio run through these alphabetical systems: A–Z, Aa–Cc (the Comedies); a–x (the Histories); aa–zz, aaa–bbb (the Tragedies).

was common and was accomplished with considerable accuracy. The advantage in it lay in the fact that, having marked in his manuscript the first and last line of every page to be printed, the compositor could (without regard to the continuity of his text) set up the type for the pages of a single forme only and so send that forme to the press immediately on completion. In folio printing, the order in which the pages were composed was normally not, 1, 2, 3, 4, but 2–3, 1–4. Pages two and three would be ready to go to the press as soon as they were set in type; pages one and four would then subsequently be set in type and sent to the press. In quarto printing, the compositor must set four pages for each forme. If he were setting *seriatim,* the compositor would set seven pages before he had the proper pages for a forme (pages 1, 2, 3, 4, 5, 6, 7 of which pages 2–3–6–7 constituted the inner forme); if he were setting by formes, he could set first either pages 2–3–6–7 or pages 1–4–5–8 (the outer forme). (The compositor might of course, when setting by formes, choose to set the pages of the forme in whatever order was most expeditious and convenient, and he often varied the order of setting where short pages, illustrations, or title pages might affect his schedule.) The composition of the pages might proceed either *seriatim* or by formes; the imposition and printing, however, could proceed, clearly, only by formes.

Large books, such as the Shakespeare First Folio, were not assembled in the manner just indicated; their composition and imposition were more complicated. For example, the First Folio is not imposed as a sequence of single sheets folded once and paged 1, 2, 3, 4 (a *folio in twos*), though this method is possible and was popular later; it is imposed as a sequence of groups of three sheets, these folded, *tucked* or *quired* one inside the other (a *folio in sixes*); each sheet is thus a part of a *gathering* or *quire*, the sheets of which have all the same signature and are numbered on the leaves in unified sequence. In this system there is an outer sheet, a middle sheet, and an inner sheet, each with its inner and outer formes. To set such a folio *seriatim*, a compositor will have to set seven pages before he can have a forme ready for the press (1, 2, 3, 4, 5, 6, 7; pages 6–7 constitute the inner forme of the inner sheet). In order to conserve type and to save time, it appears that the compositors of the Shakespeare First Folio preferred usually to cast off copy and set by formes. They proceeded, generally, in their composition from the inner forme of the inner sheet to the outer forme of the outer sheet, setting the pages in this order: 6–7, 5–8, 4–9, 3–10, 2–11, 1–12.

The practice of casting off copy and setting by formes was more than a convenience to save time; in the printing of large works, it was generally a necessity. The Elizabethan printer did not have in his shop sufficient type to set a large work from beginning to end. He was obliged by the supply of type in his typecases to set a few pages at a time and then, after those pages had been printed, to distribute the type pieces and use those very pieces over again for the next group of pages. In fact, it is possible to identify specific individual sorts—usually broken or malformed pieces—in their various appearances as they are used and reused in successive formes in the printing of a book or, for that matter, of several books or job orders. Setting by formes allowed the compositor, theoretically, to proceed with no more type than would be needed to set one complete forme (though most print shops had much more type than that), but even well-stocked shops could not set many pages *seriatim* before depleting their supplies. It is sometimes evident that the compositor did not have enough sorts of some letters even when he was setting by formes. Such shortage does not reveal itself in a complete lack of type, of course, for then the work must stop, but it does reveal itself in the lack of certain letters. For example, the letter "W," which is not common in Latin or French and so not abundant in fonts made in France, is common in English. (The specimen shown in plate 15, though printed in the Netherlands, aims at the market for Latin and French; it has no "W.")* Not infrequently, a compositor setting English in such a font, will exhaust the supply of "W" or "w"; in order to continue his work he makes good this deficiency by printing "VV" or "vv" instead of "W" or "w." Evidence of the recurrence of type pieces and of type shortage is used by modern scholars to indicate the nature of a printer's font and the order in which the pages of a particular sheet were composed. The modern practice of setting an entire book in type before printing any of it was impossible and hence unknown to the early printer.

## Imposition

When he had completed the proper pages for a forme, the compositor would place them on the imposing stone. Imposition consisted of arranging the separate pages in the proper order, guided by the catchword, and in the right direction on the stone, positioned so that the pages would print correctly on the paper—in proper

---

*Plate 10 provides a good example. The printer, having no capital "W" in his largest font, constructed one from two pieces of the letter "V," and, to make a neat join between them, he filed away the right edge of the "V" on the left.

sequence and right side up.* When the two or four or whatever number of pages were in position, the compositor would set for each page a *head title* or *running title* (a condensed title of the book or of the section within the book) and a page number for the volume (this number bore no relation to the leaf number in the sheet). He might also surround the text with *box rules,* long pieces of type that were lines that would print a kind of frame for the page of type. All of these various sorts of type would be tightly wedged with pieces of metal or wood *(furniture)* into an iron frame (the *chase*), about the size of the sheet to be printed. When the chase was firmly locked up so that the type could not wiggle about, the compositor delivered it to the pressman.

In order to save time and work, the compositor would retrieve the running titles, box rules, and furniture (the *skeleton*) of a forme after it had been printed and use them again and again as he worked his way through the book, changing the page numbers from forme to forme. Studies of these nonliterary, typographical features of a book, like the studies of compositorial preferences, guide modern scholars in preparing editions of works printed in this period.

## Presswork

After the completed chase had been placed on the bed of the press, one pressman or a young apprentice inked the type in the forme, and the other placed a sheet of paper slightly dampened (it was soon discovered that moistened paper received and held ink better than dry paper—perhaps another of Gutenberg's inventions) on the tympan and fixed it in position on the two pins (see plate 12). He then lowered the frisket over the tympan, folded the apparatus again over the type, rolled the contraption under the platen, and took the impression. When later the sheet was to be perfected it

---

*If readers wish to see how this works, they may take a sheet of paper, fold it once in a fold parallel to the short side, fold it a second time in a fold parallel to the (new) short side. They will then have a little quarto sheet. If they number the pages, from front to back 1 through 8, and then unfold the paper, they will see how the pages are disposed on each side (in each forme). They will notice also that two of the pages on each side are "upside down" and though two pages numbered consecutively may be back to back or side by side when the sheet is folded, those same two may be seemingly unconnected when the sheet is unfolded. The little sheet of paper thus marked will represent an actual *sheet* after it has been printed. To find the imposition of the *type* on the imposing stone, readers should place the same paper, now unfolded, over a new piece of paper the same size; then they should copy the numbers from each "page" of one side onto the new paper in the same order and position. The new paper will then represent the arrangement of the actual type of a single forme ready to receive the sheet to be printed. To secure the imposition of the other forme, they should turn the folded paper over, place it on another piece of paper, and repeat the process.

would be fixed again on the pointed pins of the tympan (the other side down now, of course) through the pinholes that had been made when the sheet was printed the first time; by this method, the *register* of the back of the sheet to the front of the sheet could be made exact.

When all copies of a forme had been printed, the chase was taken from the press and the type vigorously washed to remove the ink, because ink became very sticky if allowed to set too long. The type was then *distributed,* the various sorts being returned to the proper sections in cases, ready to be used again.

Though the process may seem slow, it was carried out with considerable dispatch—and not a little noise. At a normal rate of speed, a press would print about two hundred and fifty sheets per hour, creaking and groaning as the straining of the bar and platen made the timbers give and rub together. If an edition consisted of 1000 copies—1000 to 1500 copies was the normal size for a large edition in Elizabethan times—it would be possible to print all the copies desired of one forme completely in four hours and, since it was highly desirable to perfect the sheets while they were still damp from the original moistening, to print the other forme of the sheet in the afternoon—before night. Thus an edition of 1000 copies of a book containing twelve sheets—forty-eight pages in folio, ninety-six pages in quarto—could, if there were no interruptions, presumably be printed in twelve days—two weeks.

## Proofreading

The amount of care given to the proofreading of early books varied with the importance of the work being printed and the time available. The compositor read over his line in the stick, as we have seen, and he may have read over the pages of the forme on the stone; but his concern was typographical, not literary. He wished to see that his letters were all turned right side up and that the lines were all even. Some publications received no more care than this. For more important books there was a corrector of the press whose duty it was to read for sense. He received one of the first sheets of a forme to come from the press and read it over, marking errors as he saw them. He did not usually refer to the original manuscript to verify an error. If the text made sense, he let it pass; if it made no sense, he corrected it. And he corrected it as seemed appropriate to his native wit. When the corrector had made his *corrections* on the proof sheet, he returned it to the compositor who stopped the press and made the necessary changes. Uncorrected sheets already printed, the proof sheet itself, and the corrected sheets were all equally valid in the eye of the printer, and all were bound up indiscriminately in the final copies of a book to be put on sale.*

Foreign languages, the Bible, the Book of Common Prayer, and other important works might indeed be read for accuracy and fidelity to copy, but the process was cumbersome and time-consuming. Authors did not generally attend the press during the printing of their works, and proof sheets were not sent out of the print shop for correction by authors before the eighteenth century.

## The Binding of Books

Like papermaking, binding was an ancient craft, with a development and a history of its own quite apart from the invention of printing. For centuries before Gutenberg, books of blank leaves had been bound up for scribes or other keepers of records. The major change that printing occasioned in binding was quantitive, not qualitative—there were suddenly many more books to be bound than there had ever been before.

When all the sheets of a printed book had been perfected and dried, they were ready for folding, collating, and binding; but because binding was not in any way mechanized and because each book had to be treated individually as a separate item, it was not the practice to bind up all the copies of a book at the time it was printed. Instead, for reasons of economy, a few copies only were bound for sale. The remainder were kept in sheets to be sold to retail booksellers or to individuals who might wish to bind the books in some distinctive manner, or they were stored until there was demand for more copies. Some kinds of books were indeed usually sold with the entire edition already bound—schoolbooks, editions of classical authors, Bibles, prayer books, law books—but other books were sold loose in sheets or *stitched,* i.e., folded and lightly sewn or *stabbed* (in the same way that we might now staple separate sheets together along the left margin).

In order to prepare a book for binding it was necessary first to collate it. In this process, all the sheets of the book were laid out on tables in stacks, each stack consisting of all the copies of one sheet and arranged in alphabetical order of the signatures on the sheets.

---

*An unusual exception to this practice has recently come to light. A copy of Raphael Holinshed's *Chronicles of England, Scotland, and Ireland* (London, 1587) that contains hundreds of pages of proof sheets has been acquired by the Henry E. Huntington Library. The three volumes of this set were evidently compiled in the print shop while the volumes were being printed, perhaps by the proof corrector himself, who seems to have saved all the proof sheets and from those made up a set of the three volumes for himself.

# Concinnator librorum. Buchbinder.

QVisquis in Aonijs studiosus obambulat hortis,
Et studijs tempus mitibus omne locat.
Huc properet, vigili ferat atq̃ volumina dextra,
Edita Calcographus quæ prius ære dedit.

Hic ego campactos tibi leuigo ritè libellos,
Et polio, picta postmodo pelle tego.
Sericeis etiam ligis operosus adorno,
Atq̃ comas, summa qua decet arte seco.
Inter vt Aonidum vel mille volumina pulchrè
Emineat cultu conueniente liber.

C 5.                    Illu-

Plate 22
Woodcut, "Bookbinder," from *Panoplia* (Frankfurt: Hartman Schopperum, 1568).
(Courtesy of the Folger Shakespeare Library.)

A gatherer would then pass around the tables picking up one sheet from each stack; by examining the alphabet of signatures, he could be sure that he had all the sheets and that he had them in the proper sequence.

All the sheets of a single copy of the book being thus assembled, each sheet would be folded—once for folio, twice for quarto, thrice for octavo, etc., as we have already noted. By examining the numbers signed on the leaves of each sheet or gathering, the folder could be sure that he had folded the sheets in the proper direction so that the pages of the text ran consecutively.

The binder then placed the folded sheets in proper sequence on the sewing frame, the spine of the book against several strong cords or thongs; then with needle and thread he sewed the sheets to the cords, one by one successively (see plate 22). (Threads can be seen at the center folds of signatures and gatherings in modern hardcover books, for though the technique has been mechanized, the principle is unchanged.)

Then the binder pasted endpapers, usually of sturdier stock than the text paper, on the front and rear leaves of the books, and the whole was trimmed with a large cutting knife so that the three unsewn edges of the book would be smooth. In folio work the trimming was performed primarily for neatness; but for quarto and smaller books it was essential, for the folding in these formats produced folds at the top and the fore edge of the leaves and these had to be cut off before the pages could be opened.

The book with trimmed edges was now ready for casing. Covers or *boards* (made of cardboard or wood) were pasted to the endcovers, and the cords across the spine were fastened into the boards; then the book was covered with parchment or sheepskin or calfskin, occasionally with pigskin, the leather being pasted directly onto the boards. The book might be, but usually was not, marked with the title or with some decoration; the simplest markings were made by pressing heated iron stamps onto the leather *(blind tooling)*, but more elaborate ornamentation could be made by filling the designs with gold leaf *(gold-tooled)*.

The following notice accompanying the 1549 Book of Common Prayer describes the different bindings available to purchasers:

> No maner of persone shall sell this present Booke vnbounde, aboue the price of two shillynges and two pence. And bound in Forell *[parchment]* for .ii.s xd. *[two shillings and ten pence]* and not aboue. And the same bound in Shepes Lether for iii.s. iiii. pence *[three shillings and four pence]* and not aboue. And the same bounde in paste or in boordes, in Calues Lether, not aboue the price of .iiii.s *[four shillings]* the pece. God saue the Kyng.

# [ 3 ]

# Printing in England

The first record of a printed book in England derives from the purchase by an Englishman in 1467 of two copies of Cicero's *De officiis* printed by Fust and Schöffer in Mainz in 1466.* The first book printed "For the English trade" was a Latin Breviary (a prayer book) according to the liturgy used at Salisbury Cathedral, printed in Cologne in 1474. In the same city in 1471–72, William Caxton, an Englishman residing in Bruges, at the age of fifty set himself apprentice to the printer Johann Veldener in order to learn the mystery of printing. Caxton took this action, he tells us, because after he had translated into English a popular French collection of the legends of ancient Troy, so many of his friends wanted copies that he undertook to supply them "not written with pen and ink as other books be . . . [but in print so that] every man might have them at once." He learned the trade by working on the great encyclopedia by Bartholomew, *De proprietatibus rerum* (Concerning the Natures of Things), published by Veldener in 1472. Shortly thereafter Caxton returned to Bruges, where he set up a press, the first in that city, and printed his *Histories of Troy* (1474), the first book to be printed in English. Five more books were published by Caxton in Bruges—in English and in French—before in the summer of 1476, Caxton moved across the Channel to set up a bookshop in Westminster, near the south transept of the Abbey and just outside the Chapter House, in a location strategically chosen to reach and serve members of the Church, the court, and the Parliament—his customers.

---

*In a curious way, this entry is singularly important as a comment on the invention of printing: the purchaser bought *two* copies. Such a purchase is not worth a moment's thought today, but it would scarcely have been possible to purchase two copies of a manuscript book in the fifteenth century simply by walking into a shop.

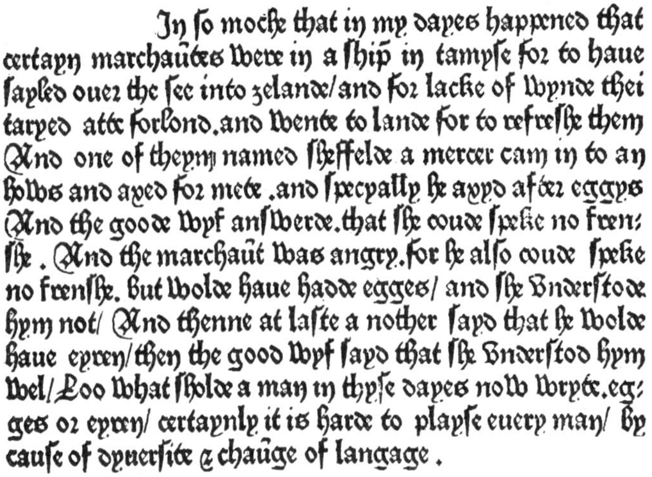
In so moche that in my dayes happened that
certayn marchaūtes were in a ship in tamyse for to haue
sayled ouer the see into zelande/and for lacke of wynde thei
taryed atte forlond.and wente to lande for to refreshe them
And one of theym named sheffelde a mercer cam in to an
hows and axed for mete .and specyally he axyd after eggys
And the goode wyf answerde.that she coude speke no fren:
she . And the marchaūt was angry.for he also coude speke
no frenshe. but wolde haue hadde egges/ and she vnderstode
hym not/ And thenne at laste a nother sayd that he wolde
haue eyren/then the good wyf sayd that she vnderstod hym
wel/Loo what sholde a man in thyse dayes now wryte.eg:
ges or eyren/ certaynly it is harde to playse euery man/ by
cause of dyuersite ⁊ chaūge of langage .

In so moche that in my dayes happened that certayn marchauntes were in a shipp in tamyse for to haue sayled ouer the see into zelande/ and for lacke of wynde thei taryed atte forlond. and wente to lande for to refreshe them And one of theym named sheffelde a mercer cam in to an hows and axed for mete. and specyally he axyd after eggys And the goode wyf answerde. that she coude speke no frenshe. And the marchaunt was angry. for he also coude speke no frenshe. but wolde haue hadde egges/ and she understode hym not/ And thenne at laste a nother sayd that he wolde haue eyren/ then the good wyf sayd that she understod hym wel/ Loo what sholde a man in thyse dayes now wryte. egges or eyren/ certaynly it is harde to playse euery man/ by cause of dyuersite & chaunge of langage.

Insomuch that in my days [it] happened that certain merchants were in a ship in Thames for to have sailed over the sea into Zeeland. And for lack of wind they tarried at Foreland, and went to land for to refresh them. And one of them named Sheffield, a mercer, came in to an house and asked for meat, and specially he asked after eggs. And the goodwife answered, that she could speak no French. And the merchant was angry, for he also could speak no French, but would have had eggs, and she understood him not. And then at last another said that he would have eiren. Then the goodwife said that she understood him well. Lo! what should a man in these days now write, eggs or eiren? Certainly it is hard to please every man, because of diversity and change of language.

Plate 24
Text from the Introduction, Caxton's translation of Vergil's *Eneydos* (Westminster: William Caxton, 1490). Gross Bastarda type (Caxton's type No. 6); and line-by-line renderings of this passage (a) literally into modern black-letter type and (b) modernized into roman. (Reproduced through the kind permission of The Henry E. Huntington Library, San Marino, California.)

own country, though he did not long enjoy his monopoly there. He was soon joined in England by John of Lithuania, who began printing in 1478; by William of Mechlin (Flanders), who began printing in 1482; and by Richard Pynson of Normandy, who began printing in 1490. All of these early printers set up their shops in London, two miles away, and Caxton's immediate successor, employed probably from the establishment of the press, Wynkyn de Worde, a native of Lorraine, moved Caxton's printing house from Westminster to London in 1500. Later printers set up their shops in Fleet Street or in the precincts and churchyard of St. Paul's Cathedral where they found in the lawyers and businessmen of the City new, and evidently profitable, markets. To Caxton's issues of polite reading matter and devotional books, they added textbooks, lawbooks, encyclopedias, liturgical books, the classics, and most of the kinds of printed matter that we see today. They also innovated: in 1495 De Worde published the first book to be printed on paper made in England (from John Tate's mill at Stevenage in Hertfordshire); in 1509 Pynson introduced roman type; in 1517 De Worde first printed in Greek characters in England, and in 1528 he printed also in Arabic and Hebrew type. As official printer to the King, Pynson printed in 1521 Henry VIII's *Assertio septem sacramentorum,* the response to Martin Luther mentioned above (see plate 7).

Before the invention of printing, the members of the book trade in England had formed themselves into a guild, the Company of Stationers. This group of scribes, illuminators, binders, and booksellers was small, and when the influx of printers came upon them, these stationers were overwhelmed. As far as can be determined now, they were not antagonistic professionally to the new men, and they seem to have assimilated themselves in the new commercial activity without protest. The scribes continued to produce manuscript books and forms for those who continued to request them—in some circles there developed a snobbish appeal in having only manuscript books; the illuminators, bookbinders, and booksellers suddenly found that they had more books to handle than they had ever dreamed of. The various craftsmen who were English learned how to work together peaceably and profitably, and, having so learned, they then began to exert pressure on the authorities to restrict the activities of craftsmen who were foreign. Their success was such that foreigners were eventually excluded by an Act of 1534. Though the English printers no doubt profited commercially from the exclusion of foreign influences, in artistic terms such exclusion was most unfortunate. In their insularity, English printers left to their own devices progressed very slowly; collections of "fine printing," for example, include no entries from English shops before the eighteenth century.

¶ LIBER GENE=
SIS, HEBRAI=
CE BERE=
SITH.
CAPVT.   I.

IN principio cre
auit deus cœlũ
et terram. Ter=
ra autẽ erat ina
nis et vacua, et
tenebꝛe erãt su=
per faciẽ abyſſi,
et ſpiritus dñi ferebatur super
aquas. Diꝛitꝗ deus: Fiat luꝛ.
Et facta eſt luꝛ. Et vidit deus
lucem quod eſſet bona, et diuiſit
ſucem a tenebꝛis, appellauitꝗ
lucem diem, et tenebꝛas noctem.
Factumꝗ eſt veſpere et mane
dies vnus. Diꝛit quoꝗ de⁹: Fiat
firmamentum in medio aquarũ,
et diuidat aquas ab aquis. Et fe
cit deus firmamentum, diuiſitꝗ
aquas quę erant ſub firmamen=
to, ab his que erant super firma
mentum. Et factum eſt ita. Uo=
cauitꝗ deus firmamentum, cœ=
lum. Et factum eſt veſpere et ma
ne dies ſecũdus. Diꝛit vero de⁹:
Cõgregentur aquæ quæ ſub cœ=
lo ſunt in locum vnum, et appa=
reat arida. Et factum eſt ita. Et
vocauit deus aridam, terram:
congregationeſꝗ aquarum ap=
pellauit maria. Et vidit deus ꝗ
eſſet bonum, et ait : Germinet
terra herbam virentem et facien
tem ſemen, et lignum pomiferũ
faciens fructum iuꝛta genus ſuũ
cuius ſemen in ſemetipſo ſit ſu=
per terram. Et factum eſt ita. Et
pꝛotulit terra herbã virentẽ ⁊ fa
cientem ſemẽ iuꝛta genus ſuũ,
lignumꝗ faciens fructum, et ha
bens vnumquodꝗ ſementem ſe
cundum ſpeciem ſuam. Et vidit
deus ꝗ eſſet bonum : Et factum
eſt veſpere et mane dies tertius.
Diꝛit autem deus : Fiant lumi=

naria in firmamento cœli, ⁊ diui
dant diem ac noctem, et ſint in
ſigna et tempoꝛa, et dies et an=
nos, vt luceant in firmamento
cœli, et illuminent terram. Et fa
ctum eſt ita. Fecitꝗ deus duo lu=
minaria magna, luminare ma=
ius vt pꝛeeſſet diei, et luminare
minus vt pꝛeeſſet nocti, ⁊ ſtellas,
et poſuit eas deus in firmamẽto
cœli, vt lucerent super terram, ⁊
pꝛeeſſent diei ac nocti, et diuide=
rent lucem ac tenebꝛas. Et vidit
deus ꝗ eſſet bonum : Et factum
eſt veſpere et mane dies quart⁹.
Diꝛit etiam deus : Pꝛoducant
aquę reptile animę viuentis,
et volatile super terram, ſub fir
mamento cœli. Creauitꝗ deus
cęte grandia, et omnem animam
viuentem atꝗ motabilem, quã
pꝛoduꝛerant aquę in ſpecies ſu=
as, et omne volatile ſecundum
genus ſuum. Et vidit deus ꝗ
eſſet bonum, benediꝛitꝗ eis, di=
cens : Creſcite et multiplicamini
et replete aquas maris, aueſꝗ
multiplicentur super terram. Et
factum eſt veſpere et mane dies
quintus. Diꝛit quoꝗ deus : Pꝛo
ducat terra animam viuentẽ in
genere ſuo, iumenta et reptilia
⁊ beſtias terrę ſecundum ſpecies
ſuas. Factumꝗ eſt ita. Et fecit
deus beſtias terrę iuꝛta ſpecies
ſuas, et iumenta et omne reptile
terrę in genere ſuo. Et vidit de⁹
ꝗ eſſet bonum, et ait: Faciamus
hominem ad imaginem et ſimi=
litudinem noſtram, et pꝛęſit piſ=
cibus maris, ⁊ volatilibus cœli,
⁊ beſtiis vniuerſæꝗ terrę, omni=
ꝗ reptili quod mouetur in terra.
Et creauit deus hominem ad i=
maginem ſuam. Ad imaginem
dei creauit illum, maſculum et
feminã creauit eos. Benediꝛitꝗ
illis deus et ait: Creſcite et mul=
mini et replete terram, ⁊ ſubiici=
A        te eam

Heb.11.a

pſ.135.a
die.10,b

pſa.135.
k.88.b

A

B

C

Infra d.
⁊ .8.c. ⁊
9.a.

D
Ma.19.a
mar.10.a
Sapi.2.d
et.10.a
Ecc.17a

pſ.135.b

Plate 25
Page from the Biblia (London: Thomas Berthelet, 1535), Gen. 1:1–28a (Vulgate).
The first Bible printed in England. (Reproduced through the kind permission of
the British Library.)

The first dayes worke. | The seconde dayes worke. | The thirde dayes worke.

The fourth dayes worke. | The fifth dayes worke. | The sixte dayes worke.

## The first Chapter.

In ye begyn nynge God created hea uen & earth: and ye earth was voyde and emptie, and darck nes was v pon the de pe, & ye sprie te of God moued vpõ the water.

And God sayde: let there be light, & there was light. And God sawe the light that it was good. Then God denyded ye light from the darcknes, and called the light, Daye: and the darcknes, Night. Then of the euenynge and mornynge was made the first daye.

And God sayde: let there be a firmament betwene the waters, and let it deuyde ye wa ters a sunder. Then God made ye firmamēt, and parted the waters vnder the firmamēt, from the waters aboue the firmament: And so it came to passe. And God called ye firma ment, Heauen. Then of the euenynge & mor nynge was made the seconde daye.

And God sayde: let the waters vnder hea uen gather thē selues vnto one place, ye the drye londe maye appeare. And so it came to passe. And God called ye drye londe, Earth: and the gatheringe together of waters cal led he, ye See. And God sawe ye it was good.

And God sayde: let ye earth bringe forth grene grasse and herbe, that beareth sede: & frute full trees, that maye beare frute, euery one after his kynde, hauynge their owne se de in them selues vpon the earth. And so it came to passe. And the earth broughte forth grene grasse and herbe, ye beareth sede euery one after his kynde, & trees bearinge frute, &

Iobas.b
Pro.8.c

Plate 26

Page from the Holy Bible (Marburg (?), 1535), Gen. 1 : 1–12a (Coverdale). The first Bible printed in English. (Reproduced through the kind permission of The Henry E. Huntington Library, San Marino, California.)

The Act of 1534 came at a crucial moment. In 1535 Berthelet published in London the first Bible to be printed in England; it was the Latin Vulgate (plate 25). In the same year the first Bible to be printed in English (the Coverdale translation), was printed, probably in Cologne or Marburg (plate 26). In 1537, Grafton, a grocer, and Whitchurch, a haberdasher, both pious men, provided a subsidy for the publication in England of the Bible in English. A translation by Tyndale, revised by Coverdale, was printed in Antwerp in 1537 and imported to England for sale. In 1539 the "Great Bible," a new English translation by Coverdale, was printed in Paris and London and published in London with the special approvals of King Henry VIII, of Thomas Cromwell, and of Archbishop Cranmer. Thus began the publication of the Bible in vernacular English, though by 1500 vernacular Bibles had already been published in German, Italian, Dutch, French, Danish, Russian, Bohemian, and Spanish. Notable later Bible translations in English were the "Geneva Bible," published first in Geneva by the Marian exiles in 1560, and the "Bishops' Bible," published by episcopal authority in 1568. The series culminated in 1611 in the "King James Bible," for over three hundred years the standard English version (plates 27 and 28).

In 1557 the Company of Stationers secured a royal charter from Queen Mary and took into its hands the control of printing and publishing. The Company specified the number of presses a printer might have, the number of copies of an edition he might print (the maximum was 1,500), and the number of journeymen and apprentices he might keep. Furthermore, the Stationers set up a Register in which a printer or bookseller might record his ownership of a title or his intent to publish it; such registering constituted a rough form of copyright. Though many books were published without entry, still the official record in the Stationers' Register provided a form of protection to the holders of copy against infringement of their rights by other printers. The Company, thus royally chartered, served as the hand of authority over the trade. The Stationers—most of whom were now printers and booksellers, the representatives of the other, old crafts having been outmaneuvered—limited the guild so as to protect it even further from the encroachment of foreign economic practices and inroads; the Crown was pleased to approve of such economic control, for that control unobtrusively provided protection from the influence of seditious or heretical ideas from foreign parts. The Company of Stationers was useful to the organization in assuring the welfare of the membership and useful to the monarchy in assuring the welfare of the commonwealth.

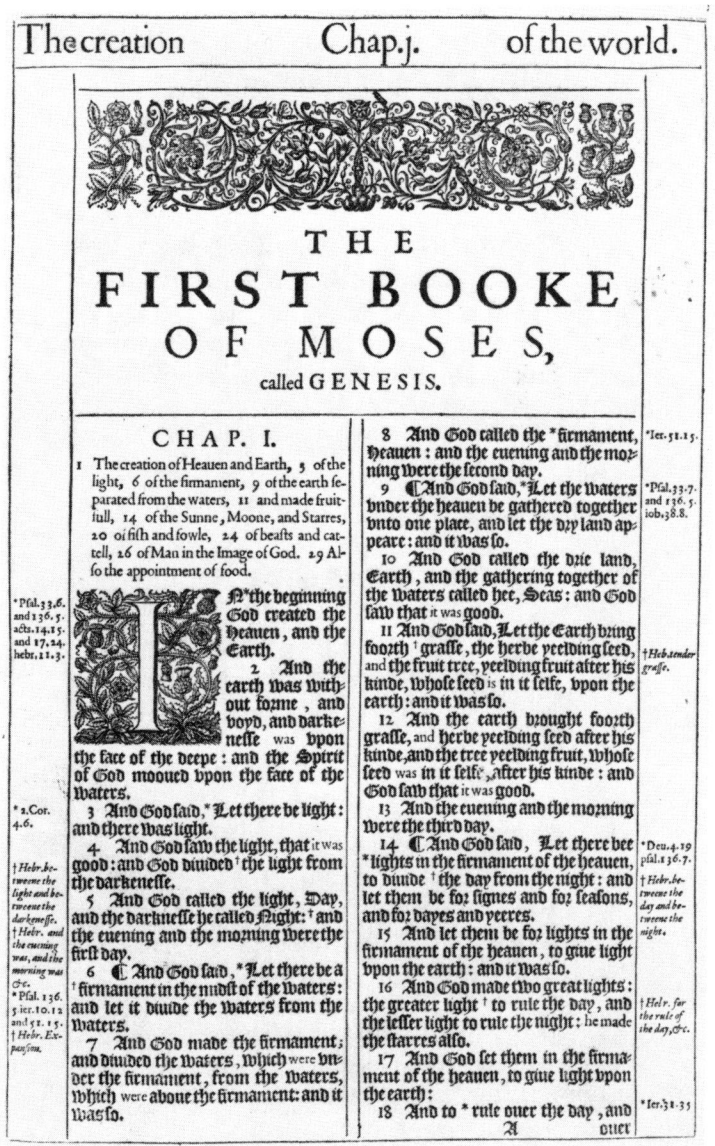

Plate 27
Page from the Holy Bible (London: Robert Barker, 1611), Gen. 1:1–18a (King James Version; The "Authorized" Version). (Reproduced from the copy in the Department of Rare Books, Perkins Library, Duke University, Durham, North Carolina, with kind permission.)

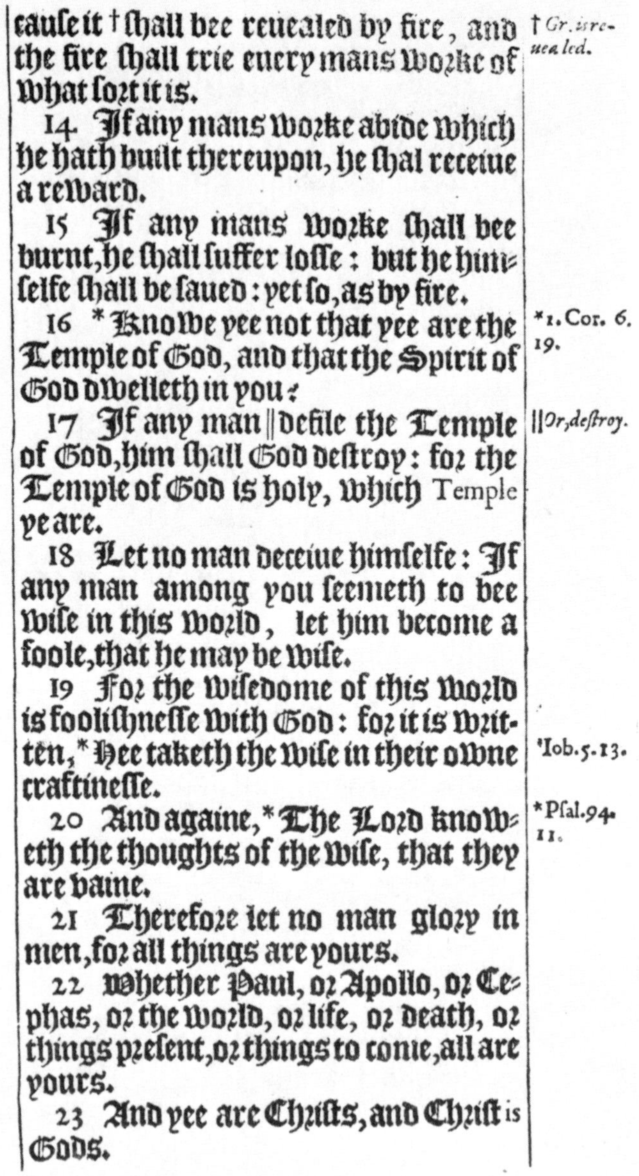

cauſe it † ſhall bee reuealed by fire, and the fire ſhall trie euery mans woꝛke of what ſoꝛt it is.

14 If any mans woꝛke abide which he hath built thereupon, he ſhal receiue a reward.

15 If any mans woꝛke ſhall bee burnt, he ſhall ſuffer loſſe : but he him-ſelfe ſhall be ſaued : yet ſo, as by fire.

16 * Knowe yee not that yee are the Temple of God, and that the Spirit of God dwelleth in you?

17 If any man ‖ defile the Temple of God, him ſhall God deſtroy : foꝛ the Temple of God is holy, which Temple ye are.

18 Let no man deceiue himſelfe : If any man among you ſeemeth to bee wiſe in this woꝛld, let him become a foole, that he may be wiſe.

19 Foꝛ the wiſedome of this woꝛld is fooliſhneſſe with God : foꝛ it is wꝛit-ten, * Hee taketh the wiſe in their owne craftineſſe.

20 And againe, * The Loꝛd know-eth the thoughts of the wiſe, that they are vaine.

21 Therefoꝛe let no man gloꝛy in men, foꝛ all things are yours.

22 Whether Paul, oꝛ Apollo, oꝛ Ce-phas, oꝛ the woꝛld, oꝛ life, oꝛ death, oꝛ things pꝛeſent, oꝛ things to come, all are yours.

23 And yee are Chꝛiſts, and Chꝛiſt is Gods.

† *Gr. is re-uea led.*

**1. Cor. 6. 19.*

‖*Or, deſtroy.*

'*Iob. 5. 13.*

**Pſal. 94. 11.*

Plate 28

Detail of Holy Bible (London: Robert Barker, 1611), the King James Version, 1 Cor. 3 : 13b–23. Compare with plates 27 and 14. (Reproduced from the copy in the Department of Rare Books, Perkins Library, Duke University, Durham, North Carolina, with kind permission.) (Reduced in size.)

# [ 4 ]

# The Printing and Publishing of Shakespeare's Works

Since no authentic literary manuscripts of Shakespeare's have been preserved, we have only the printed forms of his poems and plays from which to derive our modern editions. Critics and scholars therefore examine those printed forms, attempting to deduce from them as exactly as possible, what Shakespeare actually wrote. Though the printing history of Shakespeare's works is complicated and confused—we may almost say that no two plays have the same history—yet an analysis is possible and necessary if we wish to know what the Company of Stationers did to and for the most celebrated writer of the age.

## The Poems

Shakespeare's first printed work was a narrative poem, *Venus and Adonis,* published in 1593 in London; his next was another narrative poem, *The Rape of Lucrece,* published in 1594 (plate 29). *Venus* enjoyed nine editions in Shakespeare's lifetime; *Lucrece,* five. Both of the works carry dedications to Henry Wriothesley, earl of Southampton, signed "William Shakespeare." Both are carefully printed, apparently set up from Shakespeare's own *holograph* (the author's copy in his own hand). The poems of both volumes were printed by Richard Field, like his author, a man of Stratford; the poems were distributed through the bookseller John Harrison. Field entered the first poem in the Stationers' Register (18 April 1593); Harrison, the second (9 May 1594). It cannot be said confidently that Shakespeare

# LVCRECE.

LONDON.

Printed by Richard Field, for Iohn Harrifon, and are
to be fold at the figne of the white Greyhound
in Paules Churh-yard.    1 5 9 4.

Plate 29
Title page from *The Rape of Lucrece* (London: Richard Field, 1594). (Courtesy of the Folger Shakespeare Library.)

saw these two volumes through the press or corrected the "printer's proofs" of them, but they are both cleanly printed, and it is not unlikely that Shakespeare was attentive to their publication and anxious that the poems should appear in decent dress. Such a statement can be made of none of the plays or of the other poems. The other poems of Shakespeare were presumably published without his knowledge. *The Passionate Pilgrim* appeared in 1599 in an edition by William Jaggard, almost certainly *pirated* (unauthorized). It was reprinted once in Shakespeare's lifetime. "The Phoenix and the Turtle" appeared first in Robert Chester's *Love's Martyr* (1601). "A Lover's Complaint"—if it is Shakespeare's—accompanied the printing of the *Sonnets* in 1609.

*Shake-speares Sonnets. Never before Imprinted* were printed by George Eld for Thomas Thorpe in 1609 and were sold at the shops of William Aspley and John Wright; this was the only edition to appear in Shakespeare's lifetime (see plate 30). Some of the sonnets had circulated in manuscript in the 1590s when the vogue of sonneteering was at its height, but only two of them had been published before (nos. 138 and 144, in *The Passionate Pilgrim*). How Thomas Thorpe obtained the manuscript is unknown, but evidence deduced from the printed volume indicates that the manuscript represented a single collection and that the copy probably had been written in a single hand not Shakespeare's. Since there are relatively few errors in the typesetting of the sonnets, the manuscript must have been clear and clean, but because the provenance of the copy used by the printer is obscure, no light can be provided on the sequence of the 154 sonnets in the collection. In consequence, modern critics interested in proving one special point or another rearrange the sonnets to please their theory. Though such changes are entirely without authority, it must be conceded that the sequence as presented in Thorpe's edition yields no particular sense of overall direction or development.

In 1640 John Benson collected and published *Poems: Written by Wil. Shakespeare Gent.* Benson included 146 of the sonnets (changing the texts of some of them), the "Lover's Complaint," *The Passionate Pilgrim,* and "The Phoenix and the Turtle" as well as poems not by Shakespeare at all. This "collected" edition is a reprint of the various volumes in which the poems first appeared; in his collection, as Benson often ran several of the sonnets together, the 146 separate items were converted into 72 "poems." Benson also changed the order of the sonnets completely. The volume is of interest in showing that Shakespeare's poems had currency in the mid-seventeenth century, but it has no textual authority or significance.

# SHAKE-SPEARES

# SONNETS.

Neuer before Imprinted.

AT LONDON
By G. Eld for T. T. and are
to be folde by William Aspley.
1609.

Plate 30
Title page from *Shake-speares Sonnets* (London: Thomas Thorpe, 1609). (Courtesy of the Folger Shakespeare Library.)

## The Plays

Shakespeare wrote wholly or in part some forty plays of which we have record. About half that number were printed as separate editions during his lifetime; after his death, his fellow actors assembled his plays, including those already published, and printed (or reprinted) them in a collected edition in 1623. This date is thus useful in organizing the bibliography of Shakespeare's plays. The separate editions, because of their size (about the size and shape of a modern comic book), are called *quarto editions* or *quartos* (see plate 31); the collected edition of 1623, approximately 14″ × 9½″ in size—substantially larger than most modern books—is called a *folio edition*. The 1623 collection is called the *First Folio*.

### The Quarto Editions

Table 1 lists in the order of their publication the twenty plays published in separate editions prior to the collected edition of 1623, indicates the dates of their reprintings, and ranges them in the following categories:

A. Plays originally published in incomplete or variant texts:
  1. superseded by complete texts before 1623
  2. superseded by complete texts in 1623
  3. not superseded.
B. Plays published in complete texts before 1623:
  1. texts superseding plays in A.1
  2. texts originally complete.

A. *Plays originally published in incomplete texts.* The eleven plays published in incomplete, alternate, or variant versions are often referred to as "bad quartos" (*3 Henry VI* is actually an octavo, not a quarto), though the "badness" that they share differs markedly in degree and in kind from play to play. None of them, presumably, has any direct transcriptional link with Shakespeare's manuscript, and all derive from a version of the play written down by a reporter or a recorder after it had passed through the memories of the actors. These memorial reconstructions were prepared, we may suppose, for the legitimate purpose of the actors (to replace a lost or unavailable promptbook, for example) or for the illegitimate and unscrupulous purpose of selling the play to a printer for a few pounds. Those ten of this category that were superseded by complete or "good" editions vary throughout in details of dialogue and

# THE
# MOST LA-
## mentable Romaine
### Tragedie of Titus Andronicus:

### As it was Plaide by the Right Ho-
nourable the Earle of *Darbie*, Earle of *Pembrooke*,
and Earle of *Suffex* their Seruants.

### LONDON,
### Printed by Iohn Danter, and are
to be fold by *Edward White* & *Thomas Millington*,
at the little North doore of Paules at the
figne of the Gunne,
1594.

Plate 31
Title page from *Titus Andronicus* (London: Edward White and Thomas Millington,
1594). The first of Shakespeare's plays to appear in print (quarto format). (Courtesy
of the Folger Shakespeare Library.)

TABLE 1.   PLAYS PUBLISHED ORIGINALLY IN QUARTO
(In Chronological Order of Publication)

| Date | "Bad Quartos" | | | "Good Quartos" | | Reprints prior to 1623 |
|------|------|------|------|------|------|------|
|      | A.1. | A.2. | A.3. | B.1. | B.2. |  |
| 1594 |  |  |  |  | Titus | 1600, 1611 |
| 1594 |  | A Shrew |  |  |  | 1596, 1607 |
| 1594 |  | 2 Hen. VI |  |  |  | 1600, 1619 (Pav) |
| 1595 |  | 3 Hen. VI |  |  |  | 1600, 1619 (Pav) |
| 1597 | Romeo |  |  | 1599 |  | 1609, [1622] |
| 1597 |  |  |  |  | Rich. II | 1598, 1598, 1608 (with deposition scene), 1615 |
| 1597 |  | Rich. III |  |  |  | 1598, 1602, 1605, 1612, 1622 |
| 1598 | [L.L.L.] |  |  | 1598 |  |  |
| 1598 |  |  |  |  | 1 Hen. IV | 1598, 1599, 1604, 1608, 1613, 1622 |
| 1600 |  |  |  |  | Merchant | 1619 (Pav) |
| 1600 |  | Hen. V |  |  |  | 1602, 1619 (Pav) |
| 1600 |  |  |  |  | Much Ado |  |
| 1600 |  |  |  |  | 2 Hen. IV |  |
| 1600 |  |  |  |  | Dream | 1619 (Pav) |
| 1602 |  | Mer. Wiv. |  |  |  | 1619 (Pav) |
| 1603 | Hamlet |  |  | 1604/5 |  | 1611 |
| 1608 |  | Lear |  |  |  | 1619 (Pav) |
| 1609 |  |  |  |  | Troilus |  |
| 1609 |  | Pericles |  |  |  | 1609, 1611, 1619 (Pav) |
| 1622 |  |  |  |  | Othello |  |
|  | (3) | (7) | (1) | (3) | (9) |  |

staging from those later versions, and most of them are considerably shorter than the complete texts available in those good versions.

A.1. Three bad quartos—*Romeo and Juliet, Love's Labor Lost,* and *Hamlet*—were superseded by good quartos (B.1) soon after they appeared. (For *Love's Labor's Lost,* we must hypothesize a bad quarto of unknown date, since all that survives is a good quarto (see plate 32); this edition announces on the title page that it is "Newly corrected and augmented," a claim that has no meaning unless it refers to an earlier and incomplete edition.) The good, superseding quartos were printed from Shakespeare's final rough copies, his foul papers, but in *Romeo and Juliet* one section of about one hundred lines (1.2.46–3.34) was reprinted directly from the bad quarto, and in *Hamlet* several passages in act 1 demonstrate influence from the bad quarto in spacing and wording. The Folio texts of *Romeo and Juliet* and *Love's Labor's Lost* are mere reprints of one or another of the good quartos, but the Folio *Hamlet* seems to derive not from the quarto but from a transcript of a playhouse manuscript with, presumably, occasional consultation of the quarto.

## A
# PLEASANT
## Conceited Comedie
CALLED,
## Loues labors loft.

As it vvas prefented before her Highnes
this laft Chriftmas.

Newly corrected and augmented
*By W. Shakefpere.*

Imprinted at London by *W.W.*
for *Cuthbert Burby.*
1598.

A.2. The seven bad quartos not superseded before the Folio version are similarly diverse.

The bad quarto that corresponds to *The Taming of the Shrew* differs so markedly from Shakespeare's play that some scholars believe that it is not a version of the play at all. It has a different name, *The Taming of a Shrew,* and some of the characters have different names. The most judicious opinion is that it is probably a version much adapted and faultily remembered by the actors of Shakespeare's play as represented subsequently in the Folio. The Folio is set from Shakespeare's foul papers, without regard to the quarto. (A good quarto edition of the play, set up from the Folio was printed separately in 1631.)

*2 Henry VI, 3 Henry VI, Henry V,* and *Merry Wives of Windsor* are versions of texts deliberately shortened, presumably for performance by a limited number of players (perhaps on tour); recently it has been shown, for example, that the quarto version of *Henry V* could be played handily by eleven actors and that the act of abridging explains many of the so-called errors or faulty assignment of speeches in the quarto. The quarto itself, though a poor reflection of the Folio version, is substantially a complete and accurate rendition of the theatrical abridgement. The Folio versions of the two *Henry VI* plays seem to have been printed from a Shakespearian manuscript that had been used as a promptbook for performance; Folio *Henry V* is set from foul papers; and Folio *Merry Wives* is set from a transcript of the promptbook made by the scribe of Shakespeare's company, Ralph Crane.

*Richard III* and *King Lear* differ from the other bad quartos of this group in being full versions of the plays; no explanation of the transmission of the texts of these two has received general acceptance. The quarto version of *Richard III* is an unusually full memorial reconstruction; the Folio is probably a reprint of sections of the third and the sixth quarto, corrected by reference to an authoritative manuscript. The quarto version of *King Lear* seems to bear marks of both memorial reconstruction and literal transcription; the Folio version gives evidence that it may reflect a separate manuscript, though some critics have seen it as a reprint of a thoroughly corrected and annotated quarto. A small and growing body of authority holds that the quarto and the Folio represent two versions of the Lear story conceived by Shakespeare in forms organically different in aim and artistic perception. The two versions of *Richard III* do not have such independent lives as these, the quarto version apparently reflecting the single conception represented also in the Folio. The fact that the Folio versions of these two plays might have been set up in type from the quartos, as many scholars think, is an indication of their separateness from the others of this group, all of which are so much abbreviated or so widely variant that they could not profitably have served as the copy for the printing of the Folio.

A.3. A single play, *Pericles,* was published in 1609 in a bad quarto and not superseded: no complete text of the play exists. There are two distinct strata of composition (acts 1–2 and 3–5), and these are variously interpreted as deriving from two different authors, from two different stages in Shakespeare's own development, or from two different methods of recording the play; the quarto was also printed in two different printing houses. *Pericles* was not included in the First Folio, perhaps because Shakespeare's fellows could not find a good text, but it was added to the canon in the Folio edition of 1664, reprinted from the quarto version. The play is generally now included in the complete works of Shakespeare.

B. *Plays published in complete texts before 1623.* The nine plays originally published in complete texts are, like the three superseding quartos, usually referred to as "good" quartos. They are complete in varying degrees of accuracy, but they are all considered to have been printed in their quarto form from Shakespeare's own manuscript or a copy of it. *Titus Andronicus, Richard II, Much Ado about Nothing, 2 Henry IV,* and *A Midsummer Night's Dream* are thought to have been printed directly from Shakespeare's *foul papers* (final rough draft); *1 Henry IV, The Merchant of Venice,* and *Troilus and Cressida* are thought to have been printed from a fair copy of those foul papers (i.e., a scribe's clean copy of the rough draft); and *Othello* perhaps from the transcript of the foul papers made for a literary collector.

The quarto editions of these plays were all considered by Shakespeare's fellows to be acceptable as representing Shakespeare's finished work, and with varying degrees of theatrical or editorial attention, they were reprinted in the First Folio. *1 Henry IV, Merchant of Venice,* and *Much Ado* appear in the Folio in a state that shows minimal alteration from the quarto form; *2 Henry IV, A Midsummer Night's Dream, Troilus and Cressida,* and (perhaps) *Othello* appear in forms that reveal that before becoming copy for the Folio printer the quarto text has been altered by comparison with the foul papers or the theatrical promptbook (i.e., many readings differ—some perhaps the evidence of Shakespearean revision—and many stage directions are added). It may be that *Othello,* like *King Lear,* has survived in two artistic forms. The Folio *Titus,* though reprinted directly from the third quarto, contains a new scene (3.2) printed from a manuscript; Folio *Richard II,* printed from both the third and fifth quartos, includes a long section, the "deposition scene" (4.1 154–318), taken from a manuscript, even though the scene had already been printed (in an imperfect manner) in the fourth and fifth quartos.

*Reprints of 1619.* Among the quarto editions of Shakespeare's plays, several appear in Table 1 with the reprint notation "1619 (Pav)." These eight plays were all reprinted (with two others thought to be by Shakespeare) at the printshop of William Jaggard for Thomas Pavier in 1619, forming part of what appears to have been an attempt to issue a collection of Shakespeare's plays in quarto (see plate 33). The contents of the collection are as follows:

> *The Whole Contention between the two Famous Houses, Lancaster and*
>    *York. . . . Divided into two Parts* (i.e., *2 Henry VI* and *3 Henry VI*)
> *Pericles*
> *A Yorkshire Tragedy*
> *The Merchant of Venice*
> *Sir John Falstaff* (i.e., *The Merry Wives of Windsor*)
> *King Lear*
> *Henry V*
> *1 Sir John Oldcastle*
> *A Midsummer Night's Dream*

As the first three plays appear in consecutive pagination, it is probable that Pavier intended to print the remaining seven in the same continuing sequence. Perhaps because of intervention from the Lord Chamberlain or the Stationers Company, Pavier abandoned that scheme and produced the other plays as separate editions, substituting a false date (generally the date of the original printing) on the title page of those plays to which he did not hold copyright. So *Merchant of Venice, 1 Sir John Oldcastle,* and *A Midsummer Night's Dream* are dated "1600"; *Merry Wives* is dated "1619" (perhaps through oversight); *Lear* and *Henry V* are dated "1608." Since bibliographical inquiry has revealed that the title pages of all of the plays were printed from the same setting of type, in spite of the changes in the dates, and that all of the plays were printed on the same stocks of paper—scholars have concluded that they were printed as a unit in the spring of 1619. It was evidently Pavier's original plan to issue the whole canon in quarto form; when interrupted in this scheme, he hit upon the device of backdating the individual title pages, assuming that he could pass his new prints off as unsold copies of the first editions. But his shifting was evidently unsuccessful, for the series did not continue beyond these ten plays. Several exemplars survive, however, of the ten plays bound together as a single volume, of which one is at the Folger Library.

# THE
# Whole Contention

## betweene the tvvo Famous
### Houles, LANCASTER and
### YORKE.

*With the Tragicall ends of the good Duke*
Humfrey, Richard Duke of Yorke,
*and King Henrie the*
*fixt.*

Diuided into two Parts : And newly corrected and
enlarged.  Written by *William Shake-*
*fpeare*, Gent.

Printed at LONDON, for T. P.

Plate 33
Title page from *2* and *3 Henry VI* (London: Thomas Pavier, 1619). One of the
"Pavier quartos." (Courtesy of the Folger Shakespeare Library.)

## The Folio Editions

When he drew up his will in 1616, Shakespeare remembered his former associates in the London theater. To "my fellowes John Hemynge, Richard Burbage, & Henry Condell" Shakespeare bequeathed 26 shillings 8 pence apiece "to buy them Ringes." It is not known whether the three old actors did buy the sort of memorial rings that Shakespeare had intended for them, but in 1622, Burbage having died in 1619, Heming and Condell devised another method "to keepe the memory of so worthy a Friend, & Fellow alive, as was our Shakespeare." Thus they wrote in the dedication of the collection of plays that they sponsored, the First Folio of 1623, and in the letter "To the great Variety of Readers" they described their task:

> It had bene a thing, we confesse, worthie to haue bene wished, that the Author himselfe had liu'd to haue set forth, and ouerseen his owne writings; But since it hath bin ordain'd otherwise, and he by death departed from that right, we pray you do not envie his Friends, the office of their care, and paine, to haue collected & publish'd them; and so to haue publish'd them, as where (before) you were abus'd with diuerse stolne, and surreptitious copies, maimed, and deformed by the frauds and stealthes of iniurious impostors, that expos'd them: euen those, are now offer'd to your view cur'd, and perfect of their limbes; and all the rest, absolute in their numbers, as he conceiued them.

Much of this is publishers' blurb, of course, but basically the letter tells truth. It adverts—though not so clearly as it might have done—to three distinct groups of texts: the bad quartos, the good quartos, and the plays in manuscript. By the "maimed, and deformed" copies are probably meant the seven bad quartos (A.2), the incomplete texts of which were not superseded by good texts before 1623. "All the rest"—excepting *Pericles* (A.3)—includes the three good quartos (B.1) superseding bad quartos (A.1) and the nine original good quartos (B.2) and the plays not printed before. Table 2 lists nineteen quartos, all republished in the Folio, in the order in which they appeared in the Folio and gives the (presumed) nature of the printer's copy for each. Table 3 lists the seventeen plays in the First Folio not published previously (i.e., plays for which there are no copies extant of earlier printed editions) and gives the (presumed) nature of the printer's copy for each play.

The publication of the Folio volume was a large and expensive undertaking. William Jaggard and his son, Isaac, who had participated in the scheme of Pavier in 1619, so far from being discouraged from that experience, seem to have instigated the even

TABLE 2.  PLAYS REPUBLISHED IN THE FOLIO OF 1623
(In Order of Appearance in the Folio)

| Play | Printer's Copy for the Folio |
|---|---|
| *Merry Wives of Windsor* | Transcript by Crane |
| *Much Ado about Nothing* | Q1, adjusted from promptbook |
| *Love's Labor's Lost* | Q1 (i.e., 1598) |
| *Midsummer Night's Dream* | Q2, corrected against promptbook |
| *Merchant of Venice* | Q1, slightly edited |
| *Taming of the Shrew* | Foul papers |
| *Richard II* | Q3 and Q5, both corrected against the promptbook that contained the deposition scene (4.1) |
| *1 Henry IV* | Q5 |
| *2 Henry IV* | Uncertain |
| *Henry V* | Foul papers |
| *2 Henry VI* | Some form of Shakespeare's autograph |
| *3 Henry VI* | Some form of Shakespeare's autograph |
| *Richard III* | Q3 and Q6, the latter corrected against foul papers |
| *Troilus and Cressida* | Q1, corrected against foul papers |
| *Titus Andronicus* | Q3, with an additional manuscript for 3.2 |
| *Romeo and Juliet* | Q3 |
| *Hamlet* | Uncertain; either annotated Q2 or a transcript |
| *King Lear* | Uncertain |
| *Othello* | Uncertain |

TABLE 3.  PLAYS PUBLISHED ORIGINALLY IN THE FOLIO OF 1623
(In Order of Appearance in the Folio)

| Play | Printer's Copy for the Folio |
|---|---|
| *Tempest* | Transcript by Crane |
| *Two Gentlemen of Verona* | Transcript by Crane |
| *Measure for Measure* | Transcript by Crane |
| *Comedy of Errors* | Foul papers |
| *As You Like It* | Transcript of fair copy |
| *All's Well that Ends Well* | Foul papers |
| *Twelfth Night* | Promptbook |
| *The Winter's Tale* | Transcript by Crane |
| *King John* | Foul papers or promptbook |
| *1 Henry VI* | Transcript of foul papers |
| *Henry VIII* | Fair copy of foul papers |
| *Coriolanus* | Fair copy |
| *Timon of Athens* | Foul papers |
| *Julius Caesar* | Promptbook |
| *Macbeth* | Promptbook |
| *Antony and Cleopatra* | Fair copy |
| *Cymbeline* | Transcript (by Crane?) |

larger venture of the Folio. They presumably conferred with Heming and Condell, by 1620 the leading members of the acting company, in order to identify the canon and secure the texts of the plays; and they invited to join them in the financial risks, Edward Blount and, to a less degree, John Smethwick and William Aspley. The printing of the Folio was begun in early 1622 with the expectation that the volume would be ready by fall 1622; but the assembly of the texts was slow and difficult. The ownership of some plays was in the hands of other printers with whom the Jaggards had to negotiate. For *Troilus and Cressida* there were severe difficulties. Jaggard intended to include the play in sequence to follow *Romeo and Juliet,* but after he had begun to set it in type, he was obliged to stop— presumably because of the objection of the copyright owner, Henry Walley. The play was printed last of all, inserted out of its normal order, and not even included in the Table of Contents. That was the extreme case, but there were difficulties of other sorts with *Twelfth Night, The Winter's Tale,* and *Henry VIII.* There were delays and interruptions occasioned by other difficulties too—other printing jobs took precedence; the volume was not ready until 8 November 1623 (see plate 34). On that date it was entered in the Stationers' Register with a list of the plays not printed before (with some exceptions, table 3) for which the Jaggards now claimed ownership. William Jaggard, blind since 1613, had increasingly turned over to Isaac the operation of the shop, and it is thought that Isaac was in fact the moving spirit in the venture of the Folio. Isaac made the entry in the Stationers' Register in November, for William had died in October.

The thirty-six plays of the Folio were divided into genres at the beginning of the venture (quite different from the higgledy-piggledy of the Pavier series) and printing began with the Comedies. The order of plays within the sections of comedy and tragedy is not clear, but it seems as if the editors wished to begin and end those sections with new plays, leaving plays that had already been printed buried in the midst. In the section of history, the plays follow chronology of the reigns, but here too the first and last plays are new. The original scheme seems also to have included the plan to have the playhouse scribe provide new copy for the printer. For this reason, the first three plays are all set from transcripts by Ralph Crane, the distinctive scribe of the acting company. The plan was soon discarded.

The typesetting for the Folio was the work of perhaps eight separate compositors in the Jaggards' shop. They were men of varying ability and of varying fidelity and inventiveness. Scholars are working now to analyze the stints of the several compositors in the book

*Ex dono Willi Iaggard Typographi. aᵒ 1623*

Mr. WILLIAM

# SHAKESPEARES

COMEDIES,
HISTORIES, &
TRAGEDIES.

Publifhed according to the True Originall Copies.

*Martin Droeshout sculpsit London.*

*LONDON* -
Printed by Ifaac Iaggard, and Ed. Blount. 1623·

Plate 34

Title page from *Mr. William Shakespeares Comedies, Histories, & Tragedies* (London: Isaac Jaggard and Edward Blount, 1623). The copy of the First Folio from which this reproduction has been made (Folger No. 1) is of singular interest as it bears a notation in the hand of Augustine Vincent that the volume was a gift from William Jaggard, printer, in 1623. The printing of Shakespeare's volume was interrupted in 1622 so that Vincent's *Discovery of Errors* might be printed quickly. (Courtesy of the Folger Shakespeare Library.)

*(quantitative analysis)* and to identify the kinds of errors they are most likely to have made *(qualitative analysis)* in transmitting Shakespeare's text. Such analyses will allow them to produce texts of Shakespeare's plays more accurate than ever before.

The thirty-six plays of the First Folio established themselves as the authoritative canon of Shakespeare's work, but before we consider the transmission of that canon, we should consider other plays in which Shakespeare is thought on good evidence to have had a hand. We have already noted *Pericles,* the first of these; there are three more that should be mentioned.

*The Two Noble Kinsmen,* printed in quarto in 1634, ascribed rightly on the title page to John Fletcher and William Shakespeare, first reprinted in the second Folio edition (1679) of the works of Fletcher, has come down to us in the Fletcherian rather than in the Shake-spearian tradition. As stylistic analyses show, the play is, indeed, two thirds Fletcher's, only one third Shakespeare's.

Another collaboration with Fletcher, *Cardenio,* was produced in 1612–13. In 1653, the play was entered in the Stationers' Register to Humphrey Moseley, the publisher, who was then making a concerted effort to print the entire canon of Fletcher's plays. Since he did not publish the play then or later, we must conclude that he was entering the title as a means of reserving the copyright to himself for future use, for if he had had the manuscript in hand in 1653, he would surely have published it. (Fletcher's *The Wild Goose Chase* is a comparable example: entered by Moseley in 1646 by title but not published until 1652 when he secured the manuscript.) By the time he came to publish Fletcher's complete works in 1679, Moseley still had not secured the manuscript of *Cardenio,* and he could not include it among the fifty plays that he had assembled. The manuscript may have survived until the eighteenth century, for Lewis Theobald seems to have reworked the play and published it as *The Double Falsehood* in 1728. But since diligent search in Theobald's papers has not recovered the original manuscript, we must suppose that this collaboration of Shakespeare's is lost forever.

A third play, incomplete, is *Sir Thomas More,* to which Shakespeare, one of several collaborators, may have contributed some 168 lines. The play, never produced in Shakespeare's lifetime, was printed first in 1844 when the manuscript was discovered in the British Museum. There is general but not universal agreement that the lines in question are Shakespeare's, but the chief interest of the manuscript lies in the fact that his part of the play may have been written in Shakespeare's own hand. There is evidence that the hand-writing ("Hand D," as it is called) is indeed his, and many scholars are so anxious that it should be, that they are tempted to refer to it as if it were.

Another title, *Love's Labor's Won,* was attributed to Shakespeare in a list of his plays mentioned by Francis Meres in *Palladis Tamia* in 1598. An edition of a play by that title was printed before 1603. No copy of this edition has survived, and there are no other references to a play of this title. The most reasonable conjectures are that *Love's Labor's Won* is an alternate title for an extant play (such an alternate exists for *Twelfth Night, or What you Will*) or that *Love's Labor's Won* was an early version of *All's Well that Ends Well* or, less likely, *The Taming of the Shrew.*

To the authoritative canon of thirty-six plays, all modern editors add from this list *Pericles,* and some add also *The Two Noble Kinsmen* and *Sir Thomas More;* all wish they could add *Cardenio.* But these are exceptions; the First Folio is the accepted standard of the canon.

The First Folio was followed, nine years after its publication, in 1632, by the Second Folio, a page-for-page reprint of the first. The Third Folio, reprinting the Second, appeared in 1664 after the Restoration (plate 35). To the thirty-six plays that Heming and Condell had included, it added seven plays that had been ascribed to Shakespeare: *Pericles, The London Prodigal, The History of the Life and Death of Thomas Lord Cromwell, The History of Sir John Oldcastle, The Puritan: or the Widow of Watling Street, A Yorkshire Tragedy,* and *Locrine.* Of these, only *Pericles* has been accepted as genuinely Shakespearian; the rest, rejected by scholarly tradition, are classified—with others— as the Shakespeare "Apocrypha." The Fourth Folio, which appeared in 1685, was a reprint of the Third, with the seven additional plays. The Fourth Folio is perhaps the best of the four in terms of typography and design. As the most recent, it looks to us today, of course, as the most "modern" of the four, but it profited also from the growing awareness of members of the Stationers' Company that English books were still far behind their Continental peers in excellence of execution. It is not only an impressive volume; it is also a handsome one—praise one would be hesitant to give to any of its predecessors.

Heming and Condell tell us that they sought out the best texts of the thirty-six plays in their collection. We have seen that the copy texts used for the First Folio were more often than not Shakespeare's actual manuscripts or copies of them. Yet there are indications that some additions have been made to the texts in theatrical matters by the prompters or bookkeepers of the theater, and it is probable that the scribal copies reveal comparable additions (or subtractions) in literary matters. Furthermore, it was the understood responsibility of the men setting the type to impose some formal

# Mʀ· WILLIAM

# SHAKESPEAR'S

## Comedies, Hiſtories, and Tragedies.

Publiſhed according to the true Original Copies.

*The third Impreſſion.*

And unto this Impreſſion is added ſeven Playes, never
before Printed in Folio.

*viz.*

*Pericles* Prince of *Tyre.*
The *London Prodigall.*
The Hiſtory of *Thomas* Lᵈ *Cromwell.*
Sir *John Oldcaſtle* Lord *Cobham.*
The *Puritan Widow.*
A *York-ſhire* Tragedy.
The Tragedy of *Locrine.*

*LONDON,* Printed for *P. C.* 1664.

Plate 35

Title page from *Mr. William Shakespear's Comedies, Histories, and Tragedies* (London: Philip Chetwinde, 1664). The Third Folio, showing the titles of the seven plays newly and—with the exception of *Pericles*—falsely attributed to Shakespeare. (Courtesy of the Folger Shakespeare Library.)

standards on the author's style in matters of spelling, punctuation, and the like. It is clear, then, that the texts of the plays as they appear in the First Folio have passed through the fingers and minds of one, two, three, or more agents since Shakespeare placed them on paper.

In the First Folio, all such agents seem to have been professional men of the theater on the print shop. In the Second Folio, however, there seems to have been at work a mind that we may properly call "editorial." As the textual differences between the First and Second Folios reveal, the corrector, or editor, of the copy was a man of letters; he understood the nature of a play, he knew history and the classics, and he had an ear for metrics and verse rhythms. He corrected and improved the text before him with considerable sensitivity. Conversely, the men entrusted with the preparation of copy for the Third Folio and for the Fourth were professional proofreaders; they were interested in accuracy and typographical consistency. The latter virtue, for all its unimaginativeness, produced the clear pages of the Fourth Folio that we have already remarked. In spite of the official editors and correctors of the press, the final action lay, as it always had, with the compositors, responsible professionals who were at the same time fallible humans, whose fingers transmitted the words of Shakespeare to the printed page.

As we have seen, the publication of individual plays before 1623 was general, and many of the separate plays enjoyed frequent reprintings, a testimonial to their popularity as reading material. With the publication of the First Folio, the printing of individual plays began to diminish, and the collected volume began to claim a respect and authority that in textual matters, being more than half a reprint of earlier prints, it did not merit. But it is noteworthy that throughout the last three quarters of the seventeenth century—with the probable exception of the years of the Commonwealth—it was possible for a reader to step into a bookshop and purchase a copy of the collected plays of William Shakespeare. The First Folio had a press run of perhaps 1200 copies; later folios would have had longer runs. A reading public was developing for Shakespeare's work through the century.

When he wrote his plays, Shakespeare had one major purpose in mind—performance on the stage; and when he said, "The play's the thing," he meant not the lines of the text, but all that accompanies, sets off, and mounts that dialogue—three-dimensional actors, movement, gesture, the sights of costume, the sounds of music, even the smells of perfume or firework. The theatrical production of his book of lines was the form of publication for which he wrote, and though it is true that he wrote many more lines to his play than could be spoken in a production, he wrote them from the joy and the agony of writing, not to see them appear printed on pages in a book. Of his poems he was careful; those that he intended to publish in printed form he provided with all the apparatus of a proper book, but he seems never to have made any effort whatsoever to see his plays in print. Some of the bad quartos were replaced by good quartos; more were not. The plays had achieved their function and purpose when they received "publication" on stage.

Yet a stage performance is ephemeral, and though it is true that a spectator may retain vividly the experience of a theatrical presentation for many, many years, yet that memory must succumb to time. Before the days of film and tape, the technique of print was the only means of assuring the continuity of Shakespeare's rich achievement. Of the forty plays that Shakespeare wrote, thirty-nine transferred from manuscript to print are available in a multiplicity of copies indestructably distributed all over the world; the one that was never printed is now almost certainly lost to us forever. It is the invention of printing that has allowed posterity to assent to Ben Jonson's praise that Shakespeare was not of an age but for all time.

# Select Bibliography

## Printing, Publishing, and the Mind of Man

Barker, Nicolas. *The Oxford University Press and the Spread of Learning, 1478–1978.* Oxford: Clarendon Press, 1978.

Bennett, Henry Stanley. *English Books and Readers, 1475 to 1557.* Cambridge: At the University Press, 1952, 1969.

———. *English Books and Readers, 1558–1603.* Cambridge: At the University Press, 1965.

———. *English Books and Readers 1603–1640.* Cambridge: At the University Press, 1970.

Carter, John, et al. *Printing and the Mind of Man.* London: Cassell, 1967.

Dudek, Louis. *Literature and the Press.* Toronto: Ryerson Press, 1960.

Eisenstein, Elizabeth L. *The Printing Press as an Agent of Change: Communications and Cultural Transformations in Early Modern Europe.* New York: Cambridge University Press, 1979.

Febvre, Lucien, and Henri-Jean Martin. *The Coming of the Book.* London: NLB, 1976.

Hirsch, Rudolf. *Printing, Selling, and Reading, 1450–1550.* Wiesbaden: Harrassowitz, 1967.

Kingdon, Robert M. C. *Transition and Revolution.* Minneapolis, Minn.: Burgess Publishing Co., 1974.

McLuhan, Herbert Marshall. *The Gutenberg Galaxy.* Toronto: University of Toronto Press, 1962.

Morison, Stanley. *Politics and Script.* Oxford: Clarendon Press, 1972.

Mumby, Frank Arthur. *Publishing and Bookselling.* London: Jonathan Cape, 1930, 1954.

Rostenberg, Leona. *Literary, Political, Scientific, Religious and Legal Publishing, Printing and Bookselling in England, 1551–1700.* New York: B. Franklin, 1965.

Taylor, Archer, and Gustave O. Arlt. *Printing and Progress.* Berkeley: University of California Press, 1941.

The Times (London). *Printing in the Twentieth Century.* London: Times Publishing Co., 1930.

# The History and Spread of Printing

Bliss, Carey S. *Some Aspects of Seventeenth Century English Printing.* Los Angeles, Calif.: Clark Memorial Library, 1965.

Buhler, Curt. *The Fifteenth-Century Book.* Philadelphia: University of Pennsylvania Press, 1960.

Chappell, Warren. *A Short History of the Printed Word.* New York: Alfred A. Knopf, 1970.

Clair, Colin. *A History of European Printing.* London: Academic Press, 1976.

———. *A History of Printing in Britain.* New York: Oxford University Press, 1966.

Geck, Elizabeth. *Johannes Gutenberg: From Lead Letter to the Computer.* Bad Godesberg: Inter nationes, 1968.

Goldschmidt, Ernest Philip. *The Printed Book of the Renaissance.* Amsterdam: van Heusden, 1966.

Handover, P. M. *Printing in London: From 1476 to Modern Times.* Cambridge: Harvard University Press, 1960.

Lewis, John N. C. *Anatomy of Printing.* London: Faber & Faber, 1970.

McMurtrie, Douglas Crawford. *The Book: The Story of Printing and Bookmaking.* New York: Covico-Friede, 1957.

McMurtrie, Douglas Crawford. *Wings for Words.* New York: Rand McNally & Co., 1940.

Moran, James. *Printing in the Twentieth Century.* New York: Hastings House, 1974.

Morison, Stanley. *The Art of Printing.* London: H. Milford, 1938.

Oswald, John Clyde. *A History of Printing.* New York: Appleton, 1928.

Plant, Marjorie. *The English Book Trade.* London: Allen & Unwin, 1965.

Plomer, Henry Robert. *A Short History of English Printing, 1476–1898.* London: K. Paul, Trench, Trubner, & Co., 1900.

Pollard, Alfred W. *Fine Books.* London: Methuen, 1912.

Pottinger, David Thomas. *Printers and Printing.* Cambridge: Harvard University Press, 1941.

Rouse, Parke, Jr., and Thomas K. Ford. *The Printer in Eighteenth-Century Williamsburg.* Williamsburg: Colonial Williamsburg, 1955, 1958, 1970.

Steinberg, Sigfrid Henry. *Five Hundred Years of Printing.* 3d ed. Harmondsworth: Penguin Books, 1974.

Thorpe, James. *The Gutenberg Bible. Landmark in Learning.* San Marino, Calif.: Huntington Library, 1975.

The Times (London). "Printing and Book Production." *Times Literary Supplement,* 7 December 1943.

## Printers

Ball, Johnson. *William Caslon, 1693–1766.* Kineton: Roundwood Press, 1973.

Blades, William. *The Life and Typography of William Caxton.* Reprint New York: B. Franklin, 1965.

Caxton, William. *The Prologues and Epilogues of William Caxton.* edited by W. J. B. Crotch. London: Early English Text Society, 1928.

Childs, Edmund Lunness. *William Caxton.* London: Northwood Publications, 1976.

Deacon, Richard. *William Caxton.* London: Muller, 1976.

Duff, Edward Gordon. *A Century of the English Book Trade.* London: Bibliographical Society, 1905.

Duff, Edward Gordon. *The Printers, Stationers, and Bookbinders of Westminster and London from 1476 to 1535.* Cambridge: At the University Press, 1906.

Jennett, Sean. *Pioneers in Printing.* London: Routledge & Kegan Paul, 1958.

Needham, Paul. "The Compositor's Hand in the Gutenberg Bible: A Review of the Todd Thesis." *Papers of the Bibliographical Society of America* 77 (1983): 341–71.

Painter, George Duncan. *William Caxton.* New York: G. P. Putnam's Sons, 1977.

Plomer, Henry Robert. Wynkyn de Worde and his Contemporaries. London: Grafton & Co., 1925.

Putnam, George H. *Books and their Makers.* New York: G. P. Putnam's Sons, 1896–97.

Spencer, Herbert. *Pioneers of Modern Typography.* London: Lund Humphries, 1969.

Scholderer, Victor. *Johann Gutenberg.* London: British Museum, 1968, 1970.

Todd, William B. *The Gutenberg Bible: New Evidence of the Original Printing.* The Third Hanes Lecture. Chapel Hill, N.C.: Hanes Foundation, University Library, 1982. *See also* Needham, Paul.

## The Press

Harris, Elizabeth M. *The Common Press.* Boston: Godine, 1978.

Moran, James. *Printing Presses: History and Development from the Fifteenth Century to Modern Times.* Berkeley: University of California Press, 1973.

## Types and Type Designs

Carter, Harry. *A View of Early Typography.* Oxford: Clarendon Press, 1969.

Carter, Harry, and H. D. L. Vervliet. *Civilité Types.* Oxford: Bibliographical Society, 1966.

Condit, Lester. *Index to Roman Printing Types of the Fifteenth Century.* Chicago: University of Chicago Press, 1935.

Diringer, David. *The Illuminated Book.* London: Faber & Faber, 1958.

Dowding, Geoffrey. *The History of Printing Types.* London: Wace, 1961.

Dreyfus, John. *Type Specimen Facsimiles.* . . . With an Introductory Essay by Stanley Morison. London: Bowes & Bowes, 1963.

Duff, Edward Gordon. *Early English Printing.* New York: B. Franklin, 1970.

Gill, Eric. *An Essay on Typography.* London: Sheed & Ward, 1936.

Isaac, Francis Swinton. *English and Scottish Printing Types, 1501–1558.* Oxford: Bibliographical Society, 1930–32.

Johnson, Alfred Forbes. "Classification of Gothic Types." *The Library* 9 (March 1929): 357–80.

———. *Type Designs: Their History and Development.* London: Grafton, 1959.

McKerrow, Ronald Brunlees. *Printers' and Publishers' Devices in England and Scotland 1485–1640.* London: Bibliographical Society, 1913.

Madan, Falconer. *Books in Manuscript.* London: Kegan Paul, 1920.

Mish, Charles C. "Black Letter as a Social Discriminant in the Seventeenth Century." *Publications of the Modern Language Association* 68 (1953): 627–30.

Morison, Stanley. *First Principles of Typography.* New York: Macmillan Co., 1936.

———. *Letter Forms.* London: Nattali & Maurice, 1968.

———. *Type Designs of the Past and Present.* Cambridge: At the University Press, 1926.

———. *The Typographic Arts.* Cambridge: Harvard University Press, 1950.

———. *The Typographic Book, 1450–1935.* London: E. Benn, 1963.

Newdigate, Bernard Henry. *The Art of the Book.* New York: Studio Publications, 1938.

Plantin, Christophe. *Calligraphy & printing in the 16th Century.* Edited by Ray Nash. Antwerp: Plantin-Moretus Museum, 1964.

Proctor, Robert G. C. *The Printing of Greek in the Fifteenth Century.* Hildesheim: G. Olms, 1966.

Plomer, Henry Robert. *English Printers' Ornaments.* London: Grafton & Co., 1924.

Reed, Talbot Baines. *A History of the Old English Letter Foundries.* London: Faber & Faber, 1952.

Schonfield, Hugh J. *The New Hebrew Typography.* With an Introduction by Stanley Morison. London: Denis Archer, 1932.

Swann, Cal. *Techniques of Typography.* London: Humphries, 1969.

Updike, Daniel Berkeley. *Printing Types, Their History, Forms, and Use.* Cambridge: Belknap Press, 1951.

Vervliet, H. D. L. *Sixteenth-century Printing Types of the Low Countries.* Amsterdam: Menno Hertzberger, 1968.

Wroth, Laurence C. *Typographic Heritage.* New York: Typophiles, 1949.

## The Alphabet

Chappell, Warren. *The Living Alphabet.* Charlottesville, Va.: University Press of Virginia, 1975.

Denman, Frank. *The Shaping of our Alphabet.* New York: Alfred A. Knopf, 1955.

Diringer, David. *The Alphabet.* London: Hutchinson, 1968.

Goudy, Frederic William. *The Alphabet and Elements of Lettering.* Berkeley, Calif.: University of California Press, 1952.

Jensen, Hans. *Sign, Symbol, and Script.* New York: G. P. Putnam's Sons 1969.

Moorhouse, Alfred Charles. *Writing and the Alphabet.* London: Cobbett Press, 1946.

Scarfe, Laurence. *Alphabets.* London: Batsford, 1954.

## Ink

Bloy, Colin H. *A History of Printing Ink, Balls, and Rollers, 1440–1850.* London: Wynkyn de Worde Society, 1967.

Schwab, Richard N., et al., "Cyclotron Analysis of the Ink in the 42-Line Bible," *Papers of the Bibliographical Society of America* 77 (1983): 285–315.

## Paper

Briquet, Charles Moise. [Watermarks.] *Les filigranes. Dictionnarie historique des marques du papier des leur apparition vers 1282 jusqu'en 1600. . . .* 3d ed. A facsimile with additional material, edited by Allen Stevenson. Amsterdam: Paper Publications Society, 1968.

The Briquet Album: *A Miscellany on Watermarks.* Hilversum: Paper Publications Society, 1952.

Churchill, William Algernon. *Watermarks in Paper in Holland, England, France, . . . in the XVIIth and XVIIIth Centuries.* Amsterdam: M. Hertzberger, 1935, 1967.

Coleman, Donald Cuthbert. *The British Paper Industry, 1495–1860.* Oxford: Clarendon Press, 1958.

Green, Simon Barcham. "The Making of the Paper," *Penrose Annual,* 1976, pp. 215–18.

Shorter, Alfred H. *Paper Making in the British Isles.* New York: Barnes & Noble, 1972.

———. *Paper Mills and Paper Makers in England, 1459–1800.* Hilversum: Paper Publications Society, 1957.

Stevenson, Allen Henry. *Observations on Paper as Evidence.* Lawrence: University of Kansas Libraries, 1961.

## The Printing Process

Allen, Lewis M. *Printing with the Handpress.* 1969. Reprint. Huntington, N.Y.: R. E. Krieger, 1976.

Diringer, David. *The Hand-produced Book.* London: Hutchinson, 1953.

Gaskell, Philip. *A New Introduction to Bibliography.* New York: Oxford University Press, 1972.

Jahn, Hugo. *Hand Composition.* New York: J. Wiley & Sons, 1931.

McKerrow, Ronald B. *An Introduction to Bibliography for Literary Students.* Oxford: Clarendon Press, 1927.

Morison, Stanley. *The Art of the Printer.* New York: Simon & Shuster, 1925.

Moxon, Joseph. *Mechanick Exercises on the whole Art of Printing, 1683–4.* Edited by Herbert Davis and Harry Carter. London: Oxford University Press, 1958.

Polk, Ralph Weiss. *Elementary Platen Presswork.* Peoria, Ill.: C. A. Bennett Co., 1955.

———. *The Practice of Printing.* 1926. 3d ed., rev. and enl. by Edwin Polk. Peoria, Ill.: C. A. Bennett Co., 1952.

Young, Laurence Carvan. *Materials in Printing Processes.* New York: Hastings House, 1973.

## Binding

Davenport, Cyril J. H. *The Book: Its History and Development.* London: A. Constable & Co., 1907.

Hobson, Anthony R. A. *The Literature of Bookbinding.* London: National Book League, 1954.

Middleton, Bernard C. *A History of English Craft Bookbinding Technique.* New York: Hafner Publishing Co., 1963.

Sadleir, Michael. *The Evolution of Publishers' Binding Styles 1770–1900.* London: Constable & Co., 1930.

Samford, C. Clement. *The Bookbinder in Eighteenth-Century Williamsburg.* Williamsburg: Colonial Williamsburg, 1959.

## The Printing, Publishing, and Editing of Shakespeare's Works

Bowers, Fredson. *On Editing Shakespeare.* 2d ed. Charlottesville: University Press of Virginia, 1966.

Dawson, Giles E., and Laetitia Kennedy-Skipton. *Elizabethan Handwriting 1500–1650.* New York: W. W. Norton & Co., 1966.

Greg, W. W. *The Editorial Problem in Shakespeare.* 3d ed. Oxford: Clarendon Press, 1954.

————. *The Shakespeare First Folio.* Oxford: Clarendon Press, 1955.

Hinman, Charlton. *The Printing and Proof-Reading of the First Folio of Shakespeare.* Oxford: Clarendon Press, 1963.

Hinman, Charlton, ed. *The First Folio of Shakespeare.* Facsimile ed. New York: W. W. Norton, 1968.

Muir, Kenneth, and Michael Allen, eds. *The Original Quarto Editions of Shakespeare's Plays.* Facsimile ed. Berkeley: University of California Press, 1982.

Petti, Anthony G. *English Literary Hands from Chaucer to Dryden.* London: Arnold, 1977.

Thorpe, James. *William Shakespeare at the Huntington.* San Marino: Huntington Library, 1977.

Walker, Alice. *Textual Problems of the First Folio.* Cambridge: At the University Press, 1953.

Whalley, Joyce Irene. *English Handwriting 1540–1853.* London: Her Majesty's Stationery Office, 1969.

Wilson, Frank P. *Shakespeare and the New Bibliography.* Edited by Helen Gardner. Oxford: Clarendon Press, 1970.

## General Studies

Abbott, Craig S., and William P. Williams. *Textual and Bibliographical Studies: An Introduction.* New York: Modern Language Association, 1985.

Gaskell, Philip. *A New Introduction to Bibliography.* Oxford: Oxford University Press, 1972.

McKerrow, Ronald B. *An Introduction to Bibliography for Literary Students.* Oxford: Oxford University Press, 1927.

Spector, Stephen, ed. *Bibliographia.* New York: Garland Press, 1985.

# Index of Proper Names, Places, Printing Techniques

# Index of Proper Names, Places, Printing Techniques